The New Testament and Criticism

The New Testament and Criticism

by

GEORGE ELDON LADD

Professor of New Testament Exegesis and Theology
Fuller Theological Seminary

WILLIAM B. EERDMANS PUBLISHING COMPANY
GRAND RAPIDS, MICHIGAN

ISBN 0-8028-1680-0

First printing, April 1967
Sixth printing, June 1980

To
H. J. C.
and
P. C. D.

PHOTOLITHOPRINTED BY EERDMANS PRINTING COMPANY
GRAND RAPIDS, MICHIGAN, UNITED STATES OF AMERICA

Table of Contents

Introduction

THE PROTESTANT CHURCHES IN AMERICA ARE STILL SUFFERING from the bitter fundamentalist-modernist controversy which raged in the early twenties of the present century. The modernists, or liberals, claimed that an honest man living in the twentieth century could no longer accept the traditional orthodox formulation of the Christian faith with its unhistorical supernaturalism which contradicts the structure and character of the known world. The fundamentalists on the other hand insisted that the liberal theology had surrendered the gospel to a modern rationalistic way of thinking which was in fact "another gospel" without saving power. The liberals, claiming intellectual honesty and objectivity, insisted that the modern Christian must take his start from the modern discoveries about the nature of the world, history, and human experience and adapt the biblical message to the modern world view. The fundamentalists on the other hand argued that one must take his start from the biblical message, at the heart of which stood such fundamentals of the faith as the virgin birth, the deity of Christ, the reality of His miracles, His vicarious death, His

bodily resurrection, His second coming, and the plenary inspiration of the Scriptures. The liberals felt that these so-called
fundamentals had nothing to do with the gospel but were an
inheritance from an ancient uncritical supernaturalism from
which modern man must be set free. The fundamentalists felt
that the surrender of these essentials meant the destruction
of the Christian faith.

At the heart of this controversy stood biblical criticism. The
modernist believed that modern scholarship had at long last
achieved a true objectivity in biblical study, that a scientific
approach to the Bible demanded the rejection of the traditional
orthodox interpretation of the gospel, and that a genuinely
historical study of the Bible could penetrate through the
heavy incrustations of uncritical supernaturalism to recover
the genuine essence of the gospel which was quite compatible
with the modern scientific world view. The battle cry of the
modernists could be designated "Science." Many a devout
young man, reared in a traditional Christian environment, hearing the call of God to the Christian ministry and enrolling in
a liberal seminary, lost his traditional faith when he was taught
that modern scientific critical study of the Bible had disproved
what he had believed to be the very essence of the gospel.

This controversy projected itself beyond the limits of theological debate into the institutional life of the church. Heresy
trials were conducted; denominations were rent with bitter controversy as both liberals and fundamentalists fought to gain
control of their churches. The fact that new denominations
were founded by the fundamentalist wing, most of them with
their own theological seminaries, is an eloquent witness that at
the ecclesiastical level, the liberals won the battle. The fundamentalists had to withdraw. Not only were new denominations founded, but an independent movement flourished, made
up of churches which felt that all the major denominations
were so infected by liberalism and apostasy that any real
Christian fellowship was impossible. There were, however,
many churches and ministers who held steadfastly to the fun-

damentals of the faith, who remained in formal fellowship with their denominations out of a sense of loyalty and orderliness, even though they felt quite out of step with the marked liberal movement. Such Christians felt themselves in a real dilemma; but they hoped and prayed that God would overrule and that Christ would preserve His church.

One of the fruits of this controversy has been a strong negative attitude among fundamentalists toward biblical criticism as such. Was not biblical criticism the means by which liberalism gradually penetrated the theological seminaries, turning both professors and students away from the orthodox faith? Biblical criticism thus was often regarded as the enemy of true Christian faith and sound theology. One result of this attitude was the founding of many schools whose purpose was to teach the Bible as the Word of God and to ignore all unbelieving biblical criticism. Criticism, science, scholarship — these could be left to the liberals who had substituted human wisdom for the saving gospel. The history of the fundamentalist movement in the last few decades has therefore been characterized by a distinct separatist tendency. We have already noted this separatist movement ecclesiastically in the denominations and in the rise of the independent church movement. This same separatist tendency has influenced the fundamentalist movement at the theological and scholarly level and has resulted in a tragic dearth of first-rate scholarly production in practically all of the theological and biblical disciplines. If biblical criticism is an enemy of the Christian faith, the Bible-believing Christian can only condemn it. Fundamentalist theological literature has, therefore, been largely devotional, popular, apologetic, and defensive.

This has led the liberals to view fundamentalists as obscurantist, reactionary, and incompetent, either to be ignored or at best pitied. Many liberals are convinced that any man who believes the Bible to be the inspired Word of God cannot be truly scholarly or critical.

However, with the passing of time, we are now able to view

the entire matter in a better historical perspective. In the first place, it has become quite clear that neither the historical-critical method as it arose in German scholarship and was transplanted to America, nor the liberal theology that often accompanied it, was the product of a truly objective study of the Bible. Indeed, the modernist theology of the 1920s is today quite passé. This old-fashioned liberalism is now recognized not to have been the pure result of an unbiased and impartial study of the Scriptures but the theological product of German idealism. It has been replaced by a theology which has a far more adequate understanding of revelation, which in turn has allowed many contemporary theologians to recognize an in-escapable "supra-historical" (i.e., supernatural) element in the gospel. It has also become clear that the historical-critical method itself did not emerge as the result of open-minded, neutral, objective study of the Bible, but was motivated by rationalistic presuppositions which had no room for the biblical claim to revelation and inspiration. This fact will be illustrated in the second chapter.

Although much critical biblical study displays a negative attitude toward the biblical doctrine of divine self-revelation both in redemptive history and in the Scripture, it has shed great light on the historical side of the Bible; and these historical discoveries are valid for all Bible students even though the presuppositions of the historical-critical method have been often hostile to an evangelical view of the Bible. Contemporary evangelicals often overlook this important fact when they con-demn the critical method as such; for even while they condemn historical criticism, they are constantly reaping the benefits of its discoveries and employing critical tools.

This fact is self-evident when attention is called to it. All students of the New Testament language today, regardless of their theological persuasion, will use a modern critical text of the New Testament, whether it be the German edition edited by Erwin Nestle or the recent British edition edited by G. D.

Kilpatrick. All students will use the English translation of the famous Walter Bauer's *Griechisch-Deutsches Wörterbuch* for exegeting the New Testament.[1] All students will make use of Kittel's massive *Theologisches Wörterbuch zum Neuen Testament* now that it is being translated into English.[2] One must not forget that these everyday tools of good Bible study are the product of the historical-critical method. This fact suggests that the method as such is not hostile to an evangelical faith, but the method as employed within certain non-evangelical philosophical presuppositions about the nature of God, history, and revelation.

On the other side, it can be said that the successors to the fundamentalists of the 1920s have divided in two directions. Some have moved in the separatist direction and have shown little interest, indeed, a strengthening negative attitude toward interacting with the main stream of culture, philosophy, and theology. Their basic strategy has been that of defending their own position by the negative technique of proving all forms of liberalism are incompatible with the biblical faith. This group has assumed a basically negative attitude toward criticism as such, feeling that a critical method must be associated with a liberal theology.

There is, however, a growing number of other scholars whose theological heritage is the older fundamentalism, who are convinced of the truthfulness of the fundamentals of the Christian faith but who do not reflect the basic defensive, apologetic stance of fundamentalism. They are willing to recognize truth wherever it is found. They acknowledge their indebtedness to critical scholarship. They believe that if the traditional orthodox interpretation of the gospel is true, it should be capable of defense, not by the negative technique of attacking other posi-

---

1 See William F. Arndt and F. Wilbur Gingrich, *A Greek-English Lexicon of the New Testament* (Chicago: University Press, 1957).

2 See Gerhard Kittel and Gerhard Friedrich, *Theological Dictionary of the New Testament,* tr. by Geoffrey Bromiley (Grand Rapids: Eerdmans, 1964-) , vols. I, II, and III.

tions, but by expounding its own view in critical but creative interaction with other theologies. These modern successors of fundamentalism,[3] for whom we prefer the term evangelicals, wish, in brief, to take their stand within the contemporary stream of philosophical, theological, and critical thought.

In the area of biblical studies, this positive stance does not mean simply accepting as much biblical criticism as possible to curry favor with "the critics." This would be little more than a compromising defensive approach. The one determining factor must be: what approach does the Word of God demand of those who would understand it and correctly interpret it? It is the central thesis of this book that *the Bible is the Word of God given in the words of men in history*. As the words of men, its historical origins must be reconstructed so far as possible. This is the task of biblical criticism.

We must clearly recognize that the "historical-critical method" as the discipline has developed historically (see chapter II), and as it is often employed today, has had little room for the recognition of the Bible as the Word of God. It has insisted that in historical study, the Bible must be viewed only as the words of men. This one-sided approach has often led evangelicals to take an equally one-sided position and emphasize the Bible as the Word of God to the practical exclusion of the fact that it is also the words of men. It is the conviction of the present author that the time is ripe for a reappraisal of the entire question and for a new understanding of what an evangelical biblical criticism involves. It can no longer suffice

[3] The present author agrees heartily with his colleague E. J. Carnell that in proper historical perspective the term "fundamentalism," as applied to the contemporary scene, should be used to designate not so much a theological position as a negativistic, separatistic, apologetic stance, whereas some such term as "conservative," "orthodox," or "evangelical" serves better to designate those who desire to formulate and expound their theology in critical interaction with the entire contemporary theological scene rather than in isolation. The present author will use the term "evangelical" for this purpose. See E. J. Carnell, *The Case for Orthodox Theology* (Philadelphia: Westminster, 1959).

merely to point out the errors of the rationalistic critical approach; evangelical scholarship must offer a positive, creative approach to the problems of biblical study. A negative, defensive stance in any vital matter can never be finally convincing. The present book is a plea for a creative approach to biblical criticism by those who recognize the Bible to be the inspired Word of God. It is not designed to deal with all the problems raised by historical study nor to offer judgments on all of the critical issues. We can only select a few areas by way of illustration. We do, however, hope to suggest guidelines within which we believe an evangelical criticism ought to move.

Such an approach is not really an innovation; it merely seeks to articulate what is happening among many contemporary evangelical biblical scholars. Two very different reactions characterized the experience of most young men who were reared in an evangelical environment and deliberately exposed themselves to critical biblical studies in the university. Some accepted the (often unexpressed) presuppositions of a thoroughgoing critical method and surrendered their view of the Bible as the Word of God. Such men have commonly been characterized as "having lost their faith." Others did not feel compelled to surrender their evangelical view of the Bible, but cautiously accepted as much of the critical methodology as did not seem to conflict with their Christian faith. They sensed that a great deal of critical work involved theories and hypotheses rather than facts, and they were not ready to surrender their evangelical heritage unless established facts compelled them to do so.[4] Many of these students have become teachers and professors in evangelical colleges and seminaries and employ as

_____

[4] A sincere tribute should be paid to university teachers in the critical tradition who are truly liberal in spirit, and who may feel that their evangelical students are very slow to learn, but who, recognizing an earnestness in searching for facts, are therefore tolerant of critical conclusions different from their own.

much of the critical method in their research and teaching as
they feel established historical and literary facts demand.[5]

This book does not attempt to vindicate this procedure as a
sort of compromise between an evangelical and a critical view
of the Bible. It tries rather to clarify the issue by defending
the thesis that since the Bible is the Word of God given in the
words of men, an adequate study of the Bible demands what we
have chosen to call a historical-theological methodology.

In carrying out this objective, we must recognize distinct limitations. We can do little more than describe the several most
important kinds of critical study of the Scripture and offer a
few illustrations drawn usually from the author's special field
of study, the New Testament. Most of the illustrations involve
problems in which the author has come to positive conclusions.
It should be stressed that the same critical methods applied to
other problems might issue in negative conclusions.[6]   Our
present purpose is to defend the position that it is not enough
to refute prevailing critical views, but that evangelical scholarship must wrestle with the data and forge out its own creative
critical conclusions.

Therefore it should be clear that this book has the purpose
of discussing the validity and necessity of a proper biblical criti-

---

[5] The basic legitimacy of this approach is illustrated by the position of
a sophisticated theologian, Professor Helmut Thielicke, who defines the
role of biblical criticism to be that of "anti-criticism": to determine whether
the factual results of historical criticism contradict the content of Christian
faith (Leonhard Goppelt, Helmut Thielicke, and Hans-Rudolf Müller-
Schwebe, *The Easter Message Today* [New York: Nelson, 1964], pp. 82f.) .

[6] For example, in the author's judgment, the problem of the documentary
sources of the Synoptic Gospels and of the book of Acts embodies two
different levels of difficulty. The data of the Synoptic problem are so
distinct that the question appears to have been solved. We possess the
Gospel of Mark, and we can objectively compare it with Matthew and
Luke. However, if we did not possess the Second Gospel, it would appear
impossible to reconstruct it by critical analysis of Matthew and Luke. This
observation was made long ago by an outstanding critic, F. C. Burkitt
(*The Journal of Theological Studies*, 8 [1907], pp. 454ff.) . However, the
alleged documentary or oral sources of the Acts have been so embedded in
the book in its final form that their reconstruction can be little more than a
tentative hypothesis.

cism, not to give an "uncritical" approval of all prevailing critical theories. It must be recognized that many critical theories result from neglecting the dimension of the Bible as the Word of God. The fact that the author has tried to be positive in his approach rather than negative may lead some readers to the false conclusion that it does not matter to him to what conclusions a scholar comes so long as he uses the critical method. However, even the most radical criticism has its limitations. For as "extreme" a critic as Rudolf Bultmann, the existence of the historical Jesus is a necessity; and if historical criticism could successfully establish the "Christ-myth" theory, viz., that Jesus never really lived, Bultmann's entire theological structure would be shaken.

A significant sign in contemporary biblical study is the growing recognition that all criticism is conducted from the perspective of certain philosophical and theological presuppositions. This is as true of the most severely "objective" critic as of the extreme fundamentalist. This lays upon every scholar the demand to recognize his presuppositions and to be honestly critical of them and of himself in the light of established historical facts. The author confessedly writes from a conservative or evangelical point of view, and believes that the Bible is itself the inspired Word of God, the only infallible rule for faith and practice. His concern is, from this perspective, to illustrate to those who share his theological convictions that there is a critical method which is not hostile to this "high" view of the Bible, that in fact, the Bible demands such critical study.

The author is deeply convinced of two fundamental facts required by a careful study of the Bible: first, that the biblical doctrine of revelation demands a deed-word complex, which includes the Bible as the final term of the revealing Word of God; and second, that no one can successfully argue that the Bible was not given to us in and through human, historical media. To use the words of a contemporary evangelical scholar, "The Bible did not fall down from heaven, but originated and grew in the church of God. Books of the Bible were written according to the demands and exigencies of the times. There is nothing mechanical or artificial or inhuman about the Bible"[7] Our thesis is that this human historical dimension of the Bible demands the formulation and use of a historical-theological method of study.

The author is conscious of the fact that such a position will receive a mixed reception, both from the theological right and left. There remain many evangelicals who still hold the fundamentalist attitude, who fear any form of biblical criticism, who feel the Bible can be defended only by attacking those who do not recognize the Bible to be the inspired Word of God. To such evangelicals, the plea of the present author will likely be considered a surrender of a high view of the Bible and a capitulation before the onslaughts of unbelieving biblical criticism. But evangelical laymen as well as ministers and teachers need to understand that God, in His providence, has given the Word of God to the church through historical events and processes which cannot always be recovered. It is the task of criticism to reconstruct the historical situation so far as it is possible. Since our knowledge at many points is scanty, we often cannot accurately speak of facts, but only of probabilities, possibilities, hypotheses. This is precisely what the rationalistic critic must do. Indeed, the history of criticism is the story of the ebb and flow of critical theories, out of which have emerged many positions so well established that they may be recognized as facts. The evangelical critic must also construct his theories and hypotheses; he must constantly differentiate between facts and theories; but he will establish hypotheses which are consistent with the total biblical data, including its doctrine of revelation and inspiration.

This very procedure will raise a point of tension for many evangelicals. If the Bible is the sure Word of God, does it not follow that we must have a trustworthy word from God, not only about matters of faith and practice, but in all historical and fac-

---

[7] R. D. Preus, "The Nature of the Bible," *Christian Faith and Modern Theology*, ed. C. F. H. Henry (New York: Channel Press, 1964), p. 113.

tual questions? "Thus saith the Lord" means that God has spoken His sure, infallible Word. A corollary of this in the minds of many Christians is that we must also have absolute, infallible answers to every question raised in the historical study of the Bible. From this perspective, the "critic" is one who has surrendered the Word of God for the words of men, authority for speculation, certainty for uncertainty.

This conclusion, as logical and persuasive as it may seem, does not square with the facts of God's Word; and it is the author's hope that the reader may be helped to understand that the authority of the Bible as the Word of God is not dependent upon infallible certainty in all matters of history and criticism. Too many students have been turned from an evangelical faith because they had never learned to distinguish between a proper and an improper authority in the study of the Bible.

If this is true, it follows that the author cannot expect agreement by other evangelical scholars in all of the critical positions taken in the following chapters. It is his conviction, however, that he will find a wide agreement with his basic thesis; and it is hoped that other evangelical scholars will be stimulated to further creative critical study, and that the evangelical student in the university may find some guidance when he is confronted with an unfamiliar and seemingly hostile approach to the study of the Bible, and that thoughtful evangelical laymen will appreciate the necessity of an exacting evangelical scholarship.

On the other hand, the understanding of biblical criticism expounded in the following pages will receive a mixed reaction from those who stand to the left of the author. We have indicated above that the old liberalism has moved in a conservative direction toward a real understanding of revelation and the need of a theological interpretation. We have also pointed out that many contemporary evangelical scholars have forsaken the negativistic, defensive, apologetic attitude of the older fundamentalism and have not only been willing to learn from scholars in other traditions but desire to state their own theology in critical interaction with those with whom they disagree. This evangelical openness has often met a warm response and has often led to stimulating conversations and discussions which have been invaluable to the present author.

However, evangelicals do not always find this openness among those who do not share their view of the Bible. Many scholars are committed to what they consider to be an enlightened, scientific understanding of exegesis in such a way that the approach of the present author will simply be disposed of haughtily as "uncritical." A colleague in another seminary has spoken of the "pathological hostility" which some scholars exhibit against any high view of the Bible as the Word of God. A review of the work of my colleague, E. F. Harrison, disposes of it easily with the subjective judgment, "One has the impression that the author feels obliged to supply his students with a store of arguments with which the conservative view may be defended." It never occurs to this prejudiced reviewer that Harrison may be a competent scholar who is honestly driven to "conservative" conclusions by his evaluation of the facts. Another review speaks of the "dilemma of the new conservatives who seek to be receptive to more critical and historical methods of interpreting the Bible but who have not entirely freed themselves from an older less discerning biblicism."

The old technique of Fundamentalists was to refute their opponents by proving they were liberals; this carried its own condemnation. It is often the technique of contemporary "critical" scholars to refute their opponents by crying "conservative." This is precisely the fundamentalist technique of status by negation. Sound scholarship, regardless of theological persuasion, calls for openness without compromise, for understanding, and dialogue. It is the author's hope that the present book will find some readers who share this conviction. To them the book is addressed.

CHAPTER I

How Is the Bible the Word of God?

"I AM GLAD THAT WE FIND IN THE BIBLE THE WORD OF GOD, NOT the words of man." This statement was made in a prayer meeting recently attended by the author; and similar affirmations are frequently sounded from evangelical pulpits. The idea that such words intend to express is sound; but the thought, as here formulated, is not true but is a misleading half-truth.

The Bible *is* a compilation of the words of men. Each book of the Bible was composed by someone at a given time in a definite place, even though the author, date, and provenance are now unknown. Some books, such as the epistles of Paul, were immediately created by an individual author at a time and place which can be ascertained with relative certainty and the historical milieu and theological purpose clearly recognized. Other books, most notably the Gospels, embody the reduction to writing of a tradition which had been preserved in oral form (see chapter VI); and in some cases the facts of date, authorship and provenance cannot be ascertained with certainty. Our ignorance as to the specific background of some of the biblical books does not minimize the fact that every book has a given historical origin and from one point of view can be regarded as a purely historical, human, literary product.

The problem facing the modern evangelical is precisely this: how can the words of men be at the same time the eternal Word of God? An unhistorical answer would be: God supernaturally inspired the writers of the Bible so that they were merely mouthpieces for the Word of God. Some medieval manuscripts of the New Testament contain beautiful illustrations picturing the apostle listening to God's voice which resounds from heaven, and writing down in a book what he hears. In such pictures, the artist portrays the inspired apostle as a mere stenographer who writes down what God dictates to him; his own personality and historical situation play no role in the production of his book.

Undoubtedly, many Christians view the inspiration of the Bible in this light; but it is certainly not a modern concept. The dictation view of inspiration is already found in Second Esdras, a Jewish book written in the late first century (also called IV Ezra). The book presents Ezra in Babylon after the destruction of Jerusalem complaining that the law of Moses has been burned, and praying that God "will send the Holy Spirit into me, and I will write down everything that has happened in the world from the beginning, the things which were written in Thy law, that men may be able to find the path, and that those who wish to live in the last days may live" (II Esd. 14:22). God, in reply, tells Ezra to take five scribes or secretaries who are trained to write rapidly, and to withdraw from the people for forty days, "and I will light in your heart the lamp of understanding, which shall not be put out until what you are about to write is finished" (II Esd. 14:25). So Ezra takes the five secretaries and withdraws to the field. On the next day God says, "Ezra, open your mouth and drink what I give you to drink."

> Then I opened my mouth, and behold, a cup was offered to me; it was full of something like water, but its color was like fire. And I took it and drank; and when I had drunk it, my heart poured forth understanding, and wisdom increased in my breast, for my spirit retained its memory; and my mouth

was open, and was no longer closed. And the Most High gave
understanding to the five men, and by turn they wrote what was
dictated, in characters which they did not know. They sat forty
days, and wrote during the daytime, and ate their bread at night.
As for me, I spoke in the daytime and was not silent at night.
So during the forty days ninety-four books were written (II Esd.
14:39-44).

By this marvelous mode of inspiration, Ezra was enabled in
forty days to dictate not only the entire Old Testament, but
also a large group of extracanonical writings which were highly
valued by the Jews.

If the inspiration of the biblical books were of this nature,
many of our modern problems would never have been raised,
for the Bible would indeed be only the Word of God, and not
in any significant sense the words of men. For many centuries,
the Bible was treated as though it was only the Word of God;
and the modern discovery that the Bible is indeed the words
of men has created a tension between the theological and the
historical view of the Bible. Many critical scholars have been
so enamored of the discovery that the Bible is in fact the words
of men written within the historical process that they have
often neglected altogether the significance of the Bible as the
Word of God. The norm of modern critical study has been
deceptively and appealingly simple. The Bible is an ancient
book and must therefore be studied precisely like all other
ancient books. The critical assumptions and methodology used
in the analysis of such books as Second Esdras, the other Jewish
books of the so-called Apocrypha and Pseudepigrapha,[1] the recently discovered Dead Sea Scrolls, and all other ancient literature, Jewish or Greek, religious or secular, must be applied to
the Bible.

This is only partially true; but it *is* partially true. The purpose of this book is to illustrate the most important critical

[1] These are the two main collections of Jewish writings produced be-
tween 250 B.C. and 100 A.D. They have been published in English by R. H.
Charles, *The Apocrypha and Pseudepigrapha of the Old Testament in
English* (Oxford: Clarendon Press, 1913).

methods used in studying the Bible. These critical methods must be used because of the obvious fact that the Bible is not a magical book, but a product of history written in the words of men.

The Bible was not written like the books reputedly dictated to Ezra, in characters which the scribes did not know, but in the common languages of the ancient world. We shall point out in a later chapter that the Greek of the New Testament was not a special language created by the Holy Spirit but was basically the vernacular tongue of everyday people. The Bible must be finally studied in its original languages, Greek and Hebrew (with a few passages in Aramaic). The books of the Bible, written in very different literary styles, reflect the diversity of human authorship. Each book embodies the distinct human literary characteristics of its author. Some books are written in a very simple, easy style; others are more polished and difficult. Some have a limited vocabulary, others a far more extensive one. Most of the New Testament is written in relatively smooth Greek, but some books, such as Mark and II Peter, are rough or ponderous. Revelation is studded with intolerable Greek constructions. Obviously, the fact that the Bible is the Word of God does not mean that the human factor has been ignored nor the words of men bypassed. Thorough Bible study must employ all the paraphernalia of the linguistic, philological, and literary sciences. Although this obvious fact is admitted even in the most uncritical circles, its implications have not been understood.

To admit that the Bible is written in the words of men and must be studied as an ancient literary work is not to deny that God speaks to men day by day through the Scriptures apart from any such critical study. When I read in John 3:16, the "most beloved verse in the Bible," that "God so loved the world, that he gave his only begotten Son, that whosoever believeth in him should not perish, but have everlasting life," I do not need to ask a scholar about the meaning of the verse in order to believe, to commit myself to Christ, and to enter into the life of which the verse speaks. Furthermore, searching for and finding answers to questions of a critical kind is not the equivalent of believing and finding everlasting life. Unfortunately, critical scholarship has usually been satisfied to seek solutions to questions of this type and stops short of entering into the reality to which the Word of God witnesses. When this happens, the Word of God has indeed become only the words of men.

On the other hand, the fact that I have believed in Jesus Christ and have received the gift of eternal life ought never to prevent me from asking critical questions; indeed, I ought to be stimulated to determine as precisely as possible what the biblical language means. The scholar must ask such questions; and the intelligent layman ought to be eager for all the light he can gain from the scholar in understanding the exact meaning of the Word of God.

Why, for instance, does the RSV render the Greek *monogenes* (which the AV translates "only begotten") as "only"? Does this reflect a change in theology? What is the precise philological meaning of the Greek word *monogenes?* Does it have some subtle theological meaning — "only begotten"; or is the meaning in John 3:16 the same as in Luke 7:12; 8:42; 9:38? What is the precise theological content of "Son"? Does it indicate merely God's creativity (Luke 1:35; 3:38)? Does it have only a religious content (Ex. 4:22; Hos. 11:1; Rom. 8:14)? Does it designate Jesus as the Davidic Son of God, the messianic King (II Sam. 7:14; Psalms 2:7; 89:27, 29)? Historically considered, it is quite uncritical to assume that everywhere "Son of God" appears in the New Testament in reference to Jesus, it designates incarnate deity (see chapter VII). We believe that the use of the title in both John and the Synoptics does include more than the nativistic, religious, or messianic meanings; but this conclusion can be established only by meticulous critical study. Again, the critical student must ask about the meaning and content of everlasting (eternal) life. Is it primarily salvation in the Age to Come — the life of the resurrection, as in Daniel 12:2, Matthew 19:16, 29; 25:46? Or is it somehow a present experience, as in John 3:36? If so, how can eternal life be *both* present and future?

The devotional use of the Bible and its power to bring men into a saving relationship with God through Jesus Christ does not depend upon an answer to these questions; but the critical scholar, i.e., the careful, thorough student must raise such questions and many others: for the Bible is indeed the words of men, written in different specific historical situations and expressing the divinely given understanding of the several authors of the meaning of God's redemptive action in Israel and in Jesus of Nazareth.

This raises the question, In what sense is the Bible the Word of God? How can it be *both* the words of men and the Word of God? If the books of the Bible are given in historical situations through the words of men to meet specific historical situations, must not the Bible be studied simply as the history of human ideas about God and God's redeeming work? Is not historical criticism at the same time criticism of God's Word? To answer this question, we must consider what the Bible is, and how God revealed Himself to men.

The Bible is first of all a book of history. It records the history of the Hebrews, the story of Jesus of Nazareth, and the rise of the Christian church. The first twelve chapters of Genesis are a collection of Hebrew traditions which describe what we must designate technically as "pre-historical" times. This is not to suggest that the events in Genesis 1-11 did not happen, but only that we have no extracanonical historical evidences that they happened. By "historical evidences" we mean records, documents, archaeological evidence, and other sources of ancient information by which the historian, as a historian, can establish objectively that these events occurred. The record of Genesis 1-11 cannot take us back much beyond five thousand years before Christ; yet anthropology has proven beyond serious question that man, as we know him, has lived on this planet for scores of thousands of years. Anthropology has been unable to establish that all men have descended from a single pair — Adam and Eve. There are indeed archaeological evidences for a great flood in the Near East in pre-Abrahamic times, but the debate over whether this was a local or universal flood has raged heatedly. The existence of the main pre-Abrahamic characters, Adam, Eve, Enoch, Methusaleh, Noah, and so on, cannot be established by extrabiblical sources.

For that matter, both Abraham himself and the patriarchs are known to us in ancient sources only from the Genesis record. A generation ago strict historians were inclined to discount the historicity of the patriarchal narratives (Gen. 12-50) and to view the *history* of Israel as beginning with the Exodus or later. However, modern archaeology has shed an unexpected new light on the patriarchal period, for the discoveries at Ugarit (1928) and Mari (1933) have now given us an accurate understanding of the sociological and economic situation in the patriarchal period which corresponds remarkably with the book of Genesis. Therefore, while the historian cannot say that the existence of Abraham and the patriarchs has been objectively established, he now knows that the biblical record of the patriarchal period is in agreement with what is historically known of the times.

The Bible goes on to record the birth of the nation Israel and its history. Moses was an able leader who brought the Hebrew people out of Egypt into Palestine where they settled, first as shepherd nomads, and later as a monarchy under David, Solomon, and their successors. The main outlines of Israel's interaction with the neighboring nations — Egypt, Assyria, Babylon, and Persia have been established as historical facts. Archaeology has established that there was constant tension between the Israelitic worship of their God, Jahweh, and the worship of the Canaanite deities, Baal and Ashtaroth. The division of the nation into two parts — the northern (Israel) and southern (Judah) kingdoms — the overthrow of Israel by Assyria, the conquest of Judah by Babylon, and the restoration of a remnant of Judah in the times of Ezra and Nehemiah are established history.

The Old Testament, then, is largely a book of the traditions and history of Israel. Added to it is a collection of poetical books (Job, Psalms, Proverbs, Ecclesiastes, Song of Solomon), and a collection of prophetic writings identified with the names of prophets who preached to both Israel and Judah the will of God from the pre-exilic times of Amos (*ca.* 775 B.C.) to the post-exilic period of Haggai, Zechariah, and Malachi.

If the Old Testament records Israel's traditions, history, poetry, and prophecy, how is it also the Word of God? Are we perhaps to conclude that the Word of God is to be found only in the prophetic words, and not in the historical record? What does history have to do with the divine self-revelation? At this point we are confronted by the central feature of the biblical truth of revelation and of the role of the Bible in this divine self-revelation: God has revealed Himself to men not only in words, but first of all in acts, in deeds, in historical events. History is the vehicle of the divine self-revelation.

When God called Moses and commissioned him to lead Israel out of Egypt into Palestine, the purpose was not only the deliverance of God's people; it was also divine self-revelation. Israel would know that Jahweh is God because of His mighty acts in delivering them from bondage. "I will bring you out from under the burdens of the Egyptians, and I will deliver you from their bondage, and I will redeem you with an outstretched arm and with great acts of judgment . . . *and you shall know that I am the Lord your God,* who has brought you out from under the burdens of the Egyptians" (Ex. 6:6-7). Israel would come to know God not because He had appeared to Moses, or spoken to Moses, or given Moses a personal revelation which he in turn conveyed to the people. Israel would know God because of what He had done — His mighty acts — His saving deeds in history. The deliverance from Egypt was not accomplished by some wise plan devised by the Israelites, nor by the skillful leadership of Moses, nor by the decision of the Pharaoh; it was an act of God, a divine salvation, through which God revealed Himself to be God — the God who delivers and saves His people.

However, the revealing event was not a bare event. That is, God did not accomplish the deliverance and leave Israel to assume that He was the actor. God's works did not speak for themselves; along with the event, He gave a divine word of interpretation. God acted, and God spoke; and His word explained the event.

God told Moses what He would do; and Moses conveyed to Israel the Word of God, both before the event (Ex. 4:28-31), and after it. Moses did not try to convince the people that they were powerful, that Pharaoh was weak, or that he — Moses — had carefully worked out a plan which would set them free. On the contrary, Moses was afraid that the people would not be able to hear the Word of God in his own words (Ex. 4:1), because of his lack of eloquence or fluency of speech (Ex. 4:10). Thus the Word of God came through human words, but through a man inspired to be a prophet, who received and spoke the Word of God.

Here is the biblical mode of revelation: the revealing acts of God in history, accompanied by the interpreting prophetic word which explains the divine source and character of the divine acts. Deeds — words; God acts — God speaks; and the words explain the deeds. The deeds could not be understood unless accompanied by the divine word; and the word would seem powerless unless accompanied by the mighty works. Both the acts and the words are divine events, coming from God. In fact, it would be better to speak of the revealing deed-word event, for the two belong together and form an inseparable unity.[2]

This pattern of deed-word event is illustrated not only by the Exodus; it provides the basic structure of the biblical reality of revelation. A further illustration may suffice to reinforce this point. Both the fall of Israel before Assyria and the captivity of Judah in Babylon were historical events which the secular historian can chronicle; but in biblical history, they are viewed

[2] This approach was expounded by the present author in an essay, "The Saving Acts of God," *Basic Christian Doctrines,* ed. C. F. H. Henry (New York: Holt, Rinehart, and Winston, 1962).

as judicial acts of God in history by which He revealed Himself
as God, acting in righteousness and justice. Amos announced
the impending historical destruction of the northern kingdom
(Amos 2:6ff.) not as the result of irresistible historical forces
but as the acting of God. As God had called Israel into being as
a nation (3:1-2), so God would bring down destruction upon
a sinful, disobedient people at the hands of Assyria (3:9ff.).
Behind the historical tragedy stands God. "Therefore thus I
will do to you, O Israel; because I will do this to you, prepare
to meet your God, O Israel!" (4:12). This "day of the Lord"
(5:18-20) means exile beyond Damascus (5:27). This judgment will happen historically because God has spoken (3:8).
Even in judgment Israel is to realize through the prophetic
word that "the LORD, the God of hosts, is his name!" (4:13).

In like manner Ezekiel, speaking the Word of God after the
overthrow of Judah at the hands of Babylon, laments that
Judah's sins had profaned the holy name of God. His righteousness and justice had of necessity brought destruction and captivity upon His people for their evil ways and apostasy. However, the overthrow of God's people had resulted in the pagan
nations' mocking of Judah and her God, for it seemed that the
triumph of Babylon had proved that pagan gods were mightier
than the God of Judah. Thus God's name was profaned (Ezek.
36:20-21). However, it was neither Babylon nor her gods which
had dispersed the people of God, but God Himself (36:19).

If the prophets proclaimed to both Israel and Judah the redemptive and judicial character of God's acts in history, the
so-called historical books are no less prophetic in character.
They are not interested in Israel's history as such, but only in
Israel's history as the theatre of God's activity. The books of
Samuel, Kings, and Chronicles not only record history; they
also interpret history in terms of God's redemptive and judicial
activity. When Israel rejected God, God rejected Israel and
removed Israel from the land into Assyria so that they no longer
appeared before His sight (II Kings 17:19-23). The later captivity of the southern kingdom was due to the fierceness of God's

wrath in reaction to the apostasy and rebellion of His people (II Kings 23:26).

If God revealed Himself in redemptive power through the deliverance of Israel from Egypt and their establishment in Palestine, and in judicial power through the overthrow and captivity of both Israel and Judah, the prophets promise a further revelation of God in the future appearance of a Deliverer and messianic King. God will one day raise up a child who will be a mighty ruler, who will establish joy and peace in the world, who will crush evil and purge the earth of wickedness, who will rule with righteousness and justice (Isa. 9:2-7; 11:1-9). As a result of the coming of this messianic Ruler, "the earth shall be full of the knowledge of the Lord as the waters cover the sea" (Isa. 11:9). God's Word promises the coming of a new shepherd for His people who will feed them (Ezek. 34:23-24) and bring to them cleansing and conversion from their evil apostate ways (Ezek. 36:25-26). God will one day reveal Himself in a new dimension of salvation, not merely for the sake of His people but to make Himself known in the world. "And I will vindicate the holiness of my great name, which has been profaned among the nations . . . and *the nations will know that I am the* Lord, says the Lord God, when through you I vindicate my holiness before their eyes" (Ezek. 36:23).

This is the repeated pattern of revelation: a prophetic word from God telling what God will do and how He will reveal Himself in His saving and judicial acts; the acts of God themselves in history; and a prophetic word from God explaining the meaning of what God has done, and bringing further promises of what He will do.

The prophetic Word of God was of course first of all a spoken word. The prophets spoke to the people the contemporary word which they had received from God, interpreting what God was about to do and what He would finally do to judge and save His people. They also, however, looked to the past, to recall how God had revealed Himself in earlier times, particularly in the deliverance from Egypt and the subsequent visitation at Mount Sinai. "When Israel was a child, I loved him, and out of Egypt I called my son" (Hos. 11:1). "The LORD came from Sinai, and dawned from Seir upon us; he shone forth from Mount Paran, he came from the ten thousands of holy ones, with flaming fire at his right hand. . . . Thus the LORD became king in Jeshurun" (Deut. 33:2, 5). The past deliverances and judgments of God provided the revelation that He is God and that He will continue to deal with His people (Amos 3:1-2). God's controversy with an apostate people is grounded in the fact that they had forgotten this self-revelation in "the saving acts of the LORD" (Mic. 6:5) — what God had done for them in Egypt, how He had raised up the prophets, how He had led them through the years.

This provides us with the clue for understanding the Bible both as a record of history and as the Word of God. The Bible is both the account of God's redeeming acts, and the prophetic Word of God interpreting these acts. Its record of history is not neutral, "objective" history of the sort that a modern critical uncommitted historian would write. A historian can deal only with observable human events; he cannot, as a historian, talk about God. The biblical writers are concerned with history, but even more with the God who acts in history. Therefore the Bible is interpreted history — history understood as the vehicle of God's self-revelation and saving acts.

The New Testament is bound together by this same prophetic motif: the self-revelation of God in Jesus of Nazareth, and the divinely given interpretation of the meaning of this great historical event. The New Testament records first the ministry of Jesus, providing brief sketches of His person, mission, message, and death. However, the Gospels were not written by "neutral" or unbelieving observers, but by men who understood that the Old Testament prophetic Word of God promising a Deliverer and messianic Saviour had been fulfilled in Jesus. Uncommitted people thought that Jesus' amazing conduct indicated that He was abnormal and out of His mind (Mark 3:21) or in league with demonic power (3:22). The Gospels are both reports of events in history and also prophetic interpretations explaining who Jesus really was — the messianic Redeemer, the incarnate Son of God. They record many facts that history cannot understand or explain, for example, that Jesus was born by God's creative act in the body of Mary, that the crucified Jesus was raised from the dead.

The modern critical method of studying history, outlined in the next chapter, has assumed that all historical events must be explained by natural historical causes. From this perspective such alleged facts as the birth of a child from a virgin or a resurrection from death are simply incredible and hence excluded *ipso facto* from serious consideration. The historian tries only to explain historically, that is, humanly, how such ideas arose; he does not accept the reality and objectivity of such "supra-historical" events. However, the authors of the Gospels were convinced that the events really occurred in time and space; for here in the person of Jesus of Nazareth not only was God redemptively active among men, but God had Himself become incarnate in the person of His Son to redeem men.

The Acts of the Apostles records some of the events in the history of the men who responded to this divine revelation; the epistles, written to various churches, explain further the meaning of the person and redeeming mission of Christ, and draw implications for Christian conduct. The last book of the New Testament stands in this same stream of interpreted history and looks forward to the consummation of what God had done in Jesus, promising the final destruction of evil and the creation of a new heaven and a new earth when the entire history of God's self-revelation will achieve its divinely intended goal of a perfect human society dwelling in undisturbed fellowship with God.

The New Testament books are, like the Old Testament, both history and revelation. They record the mission of Jesus Christ and what happened as a result of His life, death, and resurrection. But they embody also the divinely given Word of God, interpreting His future coming to establish the eternal Kingdom of

God. Thus the entire Bible is both history and interpretation, deed and word.

The evangelical accepts the Bible's view of revelation. He accepts the Bible as a trustworthy record of redemptive history. He believes that such wonderful events as the incarnation, virgin birth, and resurrection of Jesus really happened in time and space. He recognizes that a secular historiography cannot explain these events; and he can understand how a rationalistic critical-historical method is offended by them. But he believes that they stand at the heart of revelation. If such events are without historical explanation or analogy, it is because in this stream of redemptive history (the Germans call it *Heilsgeschichte*), God has been pleased to be uniquely active in self-revelation.

Furthermore, the evangelical accepts the Bible's view of itself as the inspired, normative, authoritative Word of God (I Tim. 3:16; II Pet. 1:21). Revelation occurred in specific concrete events, particularly in Jesus Christ; but essential to the event are the divinely inspired words of the prophets — including the words of Jesus Himself — setting forth to their contemporaries the revelatory meaning of these events. Men were not left to guess, to speculate, to infer what the events might mean: God spoke His Word.

These events are now in the past, and the prophets are long since dead. But God in His good providence has given to men both the record of redeeming events and the corpus of the prophetic interpretation, which together constitute the Word of God, whether spoken or written. God has also given to the church the Holy Spirit, one of whose ministries is to make the events of the past revelatory and redeeming history contemporaneous with every age, to make the prophetic words written long ago living words to the modern reader. Although revelation was accomplished in past history and the prophetic word given long ago, both the redemptive events and the Word of God may become contemporary living words and events today. The death of Christ is not merely an event of ancient history;

it is the place of my redemption, and even becomes my death to my old life (Rom. 6:3-4). His resurrection is not only an event of the past which transcends the bounds of all secular historical understanding; it becomes my resurrection into new-ness of life (Eph. 2:6). The Bible is not only a historical record and the report of the divinely given Word of God interpreting the meaning of God's redemptive events to its ancient con-temporaries; it becomes contemporary with me as the Word of God, telling me who God is, how He has revealed Himself, what He has done in Jesus Christ for my salvation, and bringing me into fellowship with Him. The Bible both as history and in-terpretation is God's Word relating how God revealed Himself in history; and because it is God's inspired Word, it can become a living, inspiring word to me, bringing me into a personal experience of that to which it testifies.

Because it is history, the Bible must be studied critically and historically; but because it is *revelatory* history, the critical method must make room for this supra-historical dimension of the divine activity in revelation and redemption. A methodolo-gy which recognizes both the historical and the revelatory aspects of the Bible is what we mean by an evangelical criticism, which we shall attempt to illustrate in the chapters which follow.

CHAPTER II

What Is Criticism?

WE HAVE ARGUED IN THE FIRST CHAPTER THAT THE BIBLE IS BOTH the Word of God and the words of men. It is not a magical deposit, a book sent down from heaven, nor is it simply the record of one strand of ancient history, and therefore merely the product of historical influences. The doctrine of inspiration does not mean that the Holy Spirit dictated to the authors of the books of the Bible the very words of God so that their own personalities, literary skills, personal interests, and historical environments were completely bypassed. The biblical authors did not imagine that they received words from heaven like the Greek oracles, nor were they only recording their own religious convictions and experiences, which would be of historical interest only to twentieth-century men. The Bible is the Word of God; but is God's Word recording events in history; and since the Bible is itself the product of God's acting in historical events, it requires critical and historical study to reconstruct as far as possible the historical events through which the revelation occurred.

Recognition of this fact raises a serious question. Does not the biblical critic of whatever theological stance sit in judgment upon the Word of God rather than allowing the Word to be his judge? In brief, is the Bible as the Word of God open to any kind of criticism? If the fact that God has given men His inspired Word through historical processes requires a reverent but realistic biblical criticism, does this not by definition involve a criticism of the Bible as God's Word?

Such questions may seem naive to some readers of this book; but they are questions which vitally concern and disturb many evangelicals to whom the Bible is the inspired Word of God. Even on the level of evangelical scholarship, one sometimes is given the impression that biblical criticism is *ipso facto* an enemy of any true belief in the Bible as the Word of God. A phrase often heard is, "The critics say" — the implication being, "Away with the critics." The history and character of modern criticism provide good reason for this negative attitude, but it is our thesis that the historical character of the Bible demands a more balanced approach which makes room for a reverent criticism.

The Bible is the divinely given, inspired Word of God, the only infallible rule for Christian faith and practice. This does not mean, however, that the Bible was given to men by some sort of unhistorical, magical process, like the Book of Mormon, believed to have been discovered by Joseph Smith, who received a vision which led him to a book of golden pages buried in the ground, whose "old Egyptian" language he could translate only by the use of divinely given magical spectacles, called "Urim and Thummim." Such a supernatural book, if it ever existed, is obviously exempt from any kind of criticism.

The Bible stands in complete contrast to this Mormon tradition. The books of the Bible are capable of being studied as purely historical records. Paul, for instance, was a Christian missionary who established churches throughout Asia Minor and Greece, and who later wrote letters to his churches, dealing with specific, concrete historical problems which had arisen in the several congregations. From one point of view, the epistles can be studied solely as historical products, embodying the ideas and instructions of the greatest missionary and Christian thinker of the first century. Jesus was a man who lived, taught, and died in Palestine; and the Gospels are the records of His life, teachings, deeds, and the causes of His death. From one point of view, the Gospels can be studied as documents recording the historical traditions expressing what the believing community of A.D. 60-80 remembered of Jesus' life and believed about His person, His death, and resurrection.

The Word of God has been given to men through historical events and historical personages; and *this very fact demands historical criticism,* unless the true nature of the Bible is to be ignored. The contemporary confusion over this issue exists because of a serious failure to recognize what the Bible is, by both critical scholars and non-critical (we might better say "anti-critical") evangelicals. Both approaches — the purely human, historical, and the purely theological, revelatory — are one-sided.

"Criticism," as we would define the term, does not mean sitting in judgment on the Bible as the Word of God. Criticism means making intelligent judgments about historical, literary, textual, and philological questions which one must face in dealing with the Bible, in the light of all of the available evidence, when one recognizes that the Word of God has come to men through the words of men in given historical situations.

The Greek word from which "criticism" is derived is *krisis,* which means simply "a judgment." A "critic" in the broadest sense is a man who makes intelligent judgments or decisions about necessary questions associated with the books of the Bible. For instance, who is the author of the Gospel of Matthew? Papias (an early church father, *ca.* A.D. 130) says that Matthew wrote the Gospel in Hebrew and others translated it into Greek. Is this tradition true? Can the apostle Matthew have been the author? When was the Gospel written? Where? In Palestine, Syria, or Egypt? Why was it written? Is it an "objective" biography of the words and deeds of Jesus? If so, why does the first Gospel differ from Mark and Luke? If a Gospel is properly speaking a biography, why do we have four Gospels? Why do we not have a single, all-comprehensive biography of Jesus' words and deeds?

Do our Gospels use sources? Are they the private recollections of four separate witnesses (hardly possible, since the author of Luke does not claim to be an eyewitness), or do they represent four collections of tradition about Jesus? What is the interrelationship between the Gospels? Why are the first three Gospels similar to each other and the Fourth Gospel very different, both in style, substance, and content? Is it because of their interdependence? That is, is their similarity due to literary factors, or is it because the history of Jesus' words and deeds occurred precisely in the chronological order which appears in the first three Gospels? If the latter, why does the order of events in Matthew 4-11 differ so markedly from that in Mark? Why do Matthew and Luke contain so many passages which are almost identical word-for-word, but which are lacking in Mark?

These are only a few questions raised by a study of the Gospels; and *anyone who tries to answer these questions is a critic.* To be a critic means merely to ask questions about the authorship, date, place, sources, purpose, and so on, of any ancient literary work. The opposite of a properly "critical" approach to the study of the Bible is, therefore, an unthinking, unquestioning acceptance of tradition. To be non-critical means simply to ignore altogether the historical dimensions of the Bible and to view it as a magical book. If the Bible has come to us through historical events, persons, and situations, criticism is necessary to understand the historical process through which the sovereign God has been pleased to accomplish both self-revelation and the salvation of men.

Having said this, we must add a further word of clarification. It must be recognized that modern biblical criticism was not the product of a believing scholarship concerned with a better understanding of the Bible as the Word of God in its historical setting, but of scholarship which rejected the Bible's claim to be the supernaturally inspired Word of God. Biblical criticism as a distinct discipline has developed only in the last two centuries.

Unquestionably it has often undermined confidence in the Bible as the Word of God, and has resulted in violent controversy in the churches. In many circles today, especially in Germany but also in America, the "historical-critical method" *by definition* assumes a theological stance which regards the Bible exclusively as the words of men, in other words, as a purely human, historical product. From this presupposition the critic argues that a proper "historical method" *cannot* recognize the Bible as the Word of God, and is therefore compelled to make a negative judgment about God's redeeming revelatory acts in history. God belongs to the category of theology, not history. Hence, the only true "scientific" approach to the Bible in this perspective is one which is thoroughly human and rationalistic.[1]

This is the background for the prevailing evangelical negative stance toward the "historical-critical method" as such; and viewed in perspective, this hostility is not unjustified, for the historical-critical method, as historically developed and as it is frequently employed today, has been and is hostile to an evangelical understanding of revelation and the role of the Bible in revelation.

At this point, the reader should be advised that the definition of criticism defended here will be vigorously rejected by some scholars standing outside the evangelical tradition and dismissed with the easy judgment, "uncritical." To many scholars, the rigor of one's criticism is to be measured by the number of inauthentic verses he can find in the New Testament, particularly in the Gospels.[2] A scholar's critical acumen is often measured by the degree to which he departs from traditionally accepted positions. In other words, a scholar is not considered to be truly "critical" unless he accepts the basic naturalistic presuppositions of the modern historical-critical method, rejects every trace of the supernatural, and interprets the Bible exclusively in strict historical terms as the words of men. From this perspective, any confession that the Bible is the Word of God is *ipso facto* un-

---

[1] This rigid understanding of the "scientific" method prevails far more in Germany than in Great Britain.

[2] See Oscar Cullmann, *Heil als Geschichte* (Tübingen: Mohr, 1965), p. 172.

critical, and renders the confessor incapable of critical study. Between scholars who hold this view of criticism and evangelical scholars, there is little if any common ground for mutual inter-action and scholarly debate.

It should be clear, therefore, that the definition of terms is highly important; and it is for this reason that the present writer would suggest that the term "historical-theological criticism," which recognizes the revelatory dimension in biblical history and the revelatory nature of the Bible, is more serviceable than the more traditional term "historical-critical method," which has been developed by rationalistic scholarship.

The proponents of a thorough-going historical-critical method have insisted that historical study must be free from the restraint of any theological dogma, particularly from any doctrine of an inspired Scripture; that the biblical critic must be as open to any historical-critical conclusions as the researcher in the physical sciences must be open to the evidence of any and all facts; that any theological understanding of the Bible as the Word of God must automatically place a restraint and limitation upon the freedom of proper historical and critical investigation. How-ever, the history of criticism shows that the proponents of a purely historical method themselves have not been motivated by a completely objective open-minded approach, but have approached the Bible with distinct philosophical and theological ideas about how it should be interpreted. In other words, their critical study was dominated by certain limiting presuppositions.

Biblical criticism as a modern discipline arose in reaction to what we may call an uncritical supernaturalistic view of the Bible in post-Reformation times. What is known historically as orthodox scholasticism in seventeenth- and eighteenth-century Germany viewed the Bible almost as a magical book which was not anchored in history, but the Word of God, free from error or contradiction, without theological development or progress, possessing a single level of theological value. History was thus completely submerged in dogmatics.

The modern historical-critical method arose as a result of the effort to understand the Bible in purely historical, human terms, rejecting altogether the supernaturalism of orthodox theology. This must be plainly recognized and emphasized. Historical criticism, in its origins and development, has been, and frequently still is, the foe of any supernaturalistic understanding of the Bible as the inspired Word of God.

To place this matter in proper perspective, it will be helpful to give a brief sketch of the history of biblical criticism, various aspects of which will be enlarged upon in later chapters. Modern criticism began in the eighteenth century with the appearance of Deism in England and the Enlightenment (*Aufklärung*) in Germany, both of which reflected a rationalistic philosophy which assumed that the Bible, like all other literature, must be interpreted in terms of universal laws of human reason. The religious values in the Bible were not to be found in any divine self-revelation breaking into history but only in the timeless truths contained in the Bible; and these universal truths were to be determined by human reason. From this rationalistic perspective, miracles are simply impossible, neither could Jesus be the divine Son of God. A proper "historical" approach had to penetrate behind the Gospel portrait of Jesus as a divine being — the incarnate Son of God — to reconstruct a purely "historical" portrait, that is, a naturalistic, non-supernatural picture of Jesus of Nazareth.

One of the first of these rationalistic interpretations of Jesus was that of H. S. Reimarus, professor of oriental languages in Hamburg. Reimarus (1778) distinguished sharply between the real Jesus and the quite unhistorical portrait in the Gospels. Jesus, who can be reconstructed only from faint traces remaining in the Gospels, was only a Jew who proclaimed the imminent end of the world in a thoroughly Jewish sense. After Jesus' death, when this event had not occurred, His disciples conceived of Him as a suffering redeemer for all mankind. They stole His body from the tomb and began to proclaim His resurrection from the dead. The picture of a divine Christ in the Gospels is the product of the disciples' interpretation of Jesus as the dying Saviour and is quite unhistorical. It represents Christian faith, not historical fact.

About the same time, and guided by the same presuppositions, J. P. Gabler (1787) for the first time made a distinction between dogmatic and biblical theology. In scholastic orthodoxy the Bible had been used primarily as a textbook for dogma. Gabler insisted that historical scholarship should not be concerned about dogma but only about the history of theological ideas in the Bible. He described biblical theology as the historical discipline which traces the rise of religious ideas in Israel and sets forth what the biblical writers thought about religious matters. "Biblical theology" was really not the most accurate term to describe Gabler's effort. He was not interested in "theology," that is, the knowledge of God, but only in the history of religions, and in what men believed long ago. However, in all fairness, it should also be noted that our modern study of biblical theology as a discipline, distinct from systematic or dogmatic theology, owes its origin to rationalism, not to evangelical scholarship.

This purely historical, rationalistic approach, which assumed that the Bible must be interpreted like any other ancient literature, had led J. J. Wettstein (1751-1752) to compile an extensive collection of citations from those Jewish and pagan literary sources that provided parallels to New Testament passages. Wettstein's purpose was to help the modern interpreter of the New Testament to understand it in the same sense as its contemporaries must have done.

This initial rationalistic approach to the Bible which inaugurated the historical method was soon modified under the influence of the idealistic philosophy of Hegel (d. 1813), who interpreted history as the manifestation of absolute idea or spirit in human affairs and in the universe. Hegel's system involved a dialectical pattern of tension between one position (*thesis*) and a second position (*antithesis*), from whose interaction a third position (*synthesis*) emerged, bringing into being a new insight or aspect of reality. Hegel interpreted the history of religions in terms of this evolutionary movement from nature religions through religions of spiritual individuality to Christianity, which is the absolute religion.

Under the influence of Hegelian philosophy, F. C. Baur abandoned the rationalistic effort to find timeless truths in the New Testament and instead found in the historical movements of the early church the unfolding of wisdom and spirit. Jesus' teachings, expressing His religious consciousness, formed the point of departure. Theological reflection began over the question of the place of the law in the church; and the history of the apostolic age was interpreted in terms of the conflict over this question. Paul, the first Christian theologian, took the position that the Christian was freed from the law (thesis) · Jewish Christianity, represented by James and Peter, took the opposite position that the law was binding upon Christians (antithesis). Out of the conflict between Pauline and Jewish Christianity emerged a synthesis in the old catholic church of the second century, which effected a successful harmonization of the two contradictory positions.

Baur solved the problems of the date and authenticity of the various New Testament books in terms of their *Tendenz.* Books which clearly reflect either Pauline or Jewish theology were thought to be early; books reflecting the synthesis were late. This critical principle led Baur to conclude that only four epistles were authentically Pauline. Baur was the father of the so-called "Tübingen" school which has a continuing influence in critical studies, even though Baur's idealistic philosophy has long been superseded. Regardless of the lack of soundness of his conclusions, Baur and his influential followers did raise historical questions which all scholars must face.

A new turn in historical interpretation was made under the influence of the theology of Ritschl and his followers, who interpreted the essence of Christianity as a pure spiritual-ethical religion, proclaimed by and embodied in the life and mission of Jesus. The Kingdom of God was understood as the highest good, the ethical ideal; and the heart of religion was found in personal fellowship with God.

This theological interpretation was reinforced by the solution of the Synoptic problem (the literary interrelations between the first three Gospels). Mark was discovered to be the earliest Gospel and to have been used by both Matthew and Luke. In addition to Mark, the First and Third Gospels used another document, now lost, called Q (for the German *Quelle,* "source"), whose outlines are to be found in those numerous places where Matthew and Luke alone closely parallel each other, often in almost identical verbal form. In these two oldest literary sources, scholars of this "old liberal" school believed they had recovered the true historical Jesus, freed from all dogmatic theological interpretations. Jesus was seen as a great religious personality who taught an ideal ethical religion, which had universal validity apart from its particular historical setting. Jesus' pure ethical religion was, however, radically modified after His death by diverse theological interpretations so that the gentle prophet who had preached God's love and goodness was deified and exalted, thus becoming the object of Christian faith and preaching. This precipitated the "Jesus of history — Christ of faith" controversy which stood at the heart of the old liberal theology.

This liberal interpretation, which saw Jesus as an unsurpassed human ideal and genial ethical teacher of God's love rather than the incarnate Saviour was involved in the fundamentalist-modernist controversy in America in the 1920s and 1930s. The reconstruction of the historical Jesus was made in the name of science, modernity, and sound historical criticism, whereas the idea of a divine incarnate Saviour was identified with an outmoded prescientific supernaturalism. However, this "old liberal Jesus" is today dead, particularly in German scholarship. He is now recognized to have been not the reconstruction of an objective open-minded scholarship, but the result of superimposing German idealist theology upon the Jesus of the Gospels. It is now frequently asserted that this "liberal Jesus" never existed except in the liberal critic's reconstruction.

It should be clear that none of these critical "historical" movements was truly objective in the sense of being free from all presuppositions and completely open to the facts, wherever they might lead. "Objectivity" to them merely meant freedom from the traditional supernaturalistic understanding of biblical history. These several critical movements shared one principle in common: the critic whatever his philosophical assumption must view the Bible in terms of unbroken historical causality without "interference" or intrusions from without.

A further development of this historical method resulted from the application of the evolutionary philosophy to biblical history and gave rise to the comparative religions method (the *religionsgeschichtliche Methode*). The underlying assumption of this approach is that the religion of both Israel and the early church is an evolutionary development analogous to the Semitic and Jewish-Hellenistic religions of their respective historical milieu, and that both Old and New Testaments are therefore to be interpreted in terms of interaction with their religious environments. This approach views the Bible not as a book of theology but as a record of religious experience. It was not concerned to find in the Bible its timeless truth or theological significance, but rather to recover the history of living religious experience in terms of its own environment. Thus the theology of the Bible was quite submerged in the history of religions.

This approach led to a radically different view of Jesus from that of old liberalism, which had regarded him as a prophet of ethical idealism. Albert Schweitzer developed a thesis already expounded by J. Weiss (and more than a century earlier by Reimarus) portraying Jesus as a Jew with a single message: the imminent end of the world. Scientific researchers had discovered the historical significance in Judaism of such "apocalyptic" writings as Enoch, the Apocalypse of Baruch, and IV Ezra (II Esdras in the Apocrypha), in which the Kingdom of God was conceived of exclusively as an imminent supernatural act of God breaking off human history and transforming the world into the Kingdom of God. Schweitzer held that this apocalyptic coming of

God's Kingdom was Jesus' only concern; that He conceived of Himself as destined by God to be exalted to heaven as the heavenly Son of Man who will come on the clouds to judge the world and inaugurate the apocalyptic kingdom. Schweitzer's "historical Jesus" was, therefore, according to Schweitzer's own assertion a stranger to the modern man, whose views of history and the universe no longer allow him to believe that the world will come to its end by the appearance of a heavenly Son of Man to inaugurate the perfected Kingdom of God. According to Schweitzer, Jesus died in disillusionment; and Schweitzer's historical Jesus is disillusioning for modern religion and can no longer provide a historical basis for Christian faith. Historically, Jesus belongs to first-century Judaism and has no relevance for the modern man.

As the comparative religions school interpreted Jesus in terms of Jewish apocalyptic, it often interpreted Paul in terms of the Hellenistic religions prevalent in the Graeco-Roman world. The ancient Mediterranean world was full of cultic "mystery" religions which worshipped various ancient nature deities as heavenly "lords." By the performance of certain cultic acts, such as ablutions, sacred meals, the worshipper believed himself to be personally identified with the deity and thus assured of personal immortality. W. Bousset made classic the view that the Palestinian church was thoroughly Jewish in outlook, worshipping Jesus as a man who had been exalted to God's right hand as the heavenly Son of Man who was to come to earth in glory. Only when the church took root in the Hellenistic world, in Syrian Antioch (Acts 11:20ff.), was Jesus for the first time worshipped as a present heavenly divine being, Lord. In Christian faith, the Jewish Son of Man was interpreted against a pagan background and became the Hellenistic divine Lord. Paul was interpreted as more a Greek than a Jew. The center of Paul's belief in Christ was the heavenly Lord patterned after the pagan cults, and Pauline sacraments, baptism and the Lord's Supper were understood as adaptations of the cultic rites of the mystery religions by which the worshipper was identified with the Lord in his death and resurrection and thus was made partaker of his life.

The *religionsgeschichtliche* interpretation dominated biblical scholarship, particularly in Germany, for more than two decades. In contemporary German scholarship, it has been combined with another philosophical presupposition, that of existentialism, which has given rise to the most influential recent critical movement in German New Testament studies. This movement has centered around the name of Rudolf Bultmann, now retired, but for thirty years professor in Marburg, and teacher of the most famed New Testament scholars in contemporary Germany.

Bultmann frankly admits his presuppositions, which are twofold: historical and philosophical. As a historian, Bultmann candidly rejects the biblical world view, which he insists is intolerable in the twentieth century. No intelligent and honest man can believe in a pre-existent deity who becomes incarnate by way of a virgin birth, who performs nature miracles, who dies a substitutionary death, who rises bodily from the grave and ascends to heaven, who will return to earth visibly to judge the world and inaugurate the Kingdom of God. Neither can the modern historian believe in a God who acts directly in history. History, for Bultmann, is a closed unbroken nexus of causes and results and must be interpreted in such terms. Thus Bultmann, as a historian, believes that the Christian gospel has no word about the goal of history. All such ideas, which appear to be the center of the biblical proclamation of salvation, Bultmann calls mythological, that is, ancient human expressions about belief in the world of God.

At this point, Bultmann stands on the same strictly "historical" platform as the rationalists and the old liberals. He also employs the *religionsgeschichtliche* method to reconstruct the historical development of belief in Jesus. Jesus Himself was, as Schweitzer thought, a Jewish apocalyptic prophet announcing the imminent end of the world — an event which did not and cannot occur. The Jewish church believed that He was

exalted to heaven as the heavenly Son of Man who would return shortly to earth for judgment. The Hellenistic church interpreted Him as a gnostic divine being who came to earth and as
a dying and rising cultic Lord, exalted in heaven. All of this
is mythology, without literal significance for the modern mind.[3]

Bultmann's difference from the old liberals lies in the fact
that he does not find the essence of the gospel in a diluted version of the prophetic teachings of the critically reconstructed
"historical" Jesus, but in a reinterpretation of the New Testament mythology. The place of God's redemptive acting is not
in the events of past history but in my human existence, in my
historicity. The gospel is not a recital of what God did in Jesus
of Nazareth; it is a proclamation of what God does to me here
and now. Thus the biblical mythology of the substitutionary
atoning death of Christ, His bodily resurrection, His second coming, and of the eschatological Kingdom of God must be "demy-
thologized." The death of Christ in the preaching of the gospel
is *my* death; I die to my old life of pride and worldliness. The
resurrection is *my* resurrection; I rise to a new life of complete faith and trust in God instead of in the world. The new
world to be inaugurated by the second coming of Christ is the
new world of my Christian experience (Bultmann would prefer to say the new world of my authentic existence, for "experience" carries too subjective overtones to please him). The
Christian concepts of new birth, eternal life, justification, salvation, etc., must be interpreted in terms of modern existential
philosophy, which Bultmann believes embodies the real intent of
the New Testament gospel. Thus whereas liberalism found its
gospel in the assured teachings of the historical Jesus, Bultmann's gospel is cut loose from New Testament history and is
grounded in contemporary preaching. Bultmann, therefore, can
be a radical historical critic but at the same time can believe
he has not impaired the heart of the gospel. Indeed, one of his
deepest convictions is that the gospel of authentic existence must

[3] This rather involved historical reconstruction will be discussed at greater
length in chapter VIII.

be cut loose from dependence upon history, for otherwise the believer places his faith in history or in the historian, not in God.

The preceding survey is obviously not meant to be comprehensive, but its selection of some of the most important philosophical influences upon New Testament criticism has illustrated that the oft-vaunted claim to pure objectivity and freedom from prejudice is not accurate. It has illustrated the fact that underlying the ebb and flow of successive schools of criticism is to be found the continuing theological assumption that the nature of God and history is such that a proper critical method can make no room for the immediate acting of God in history, that is, that the supernatural must be dispensed with. For this reason many evangelicals have felt, with apparent justification, that biblical criticism *per se* is and must be an enemy of sound evangelical faith.

However, two further observations are necessary. First, there have been many scholars within the broad critical tradition who have not shared its thorough-going historicism. In other words, many scholars have used the historical-critical method but have recognized its presuppositions and have insisted on the validity of a higher dimension in the New Testament. To illustrate, E. H. Hoskyns and Noel Davey argued that *The Riddle of the New Testament* (1931) is the consistent witness of the entire New Testament that God acted to reveal Himself for man's salvation in the historical Jesus. The critical method, they insisted, has clearly revealed the living unity of the New Testament documents; and the historian is compelled to state that both the unity and the uniqueness of this claim are historical facts. This claim, while occurring in history, transcends history, for it demands of the historian what he cannot give *as a scientist*: a theological judgment of ultimate significance. In the last three decades, an extensive literature has been produced from this point of view; and while such scholars may stop short of acknowledging the Bible as the inspired Word of God, they are far from a radical historicism, and they recognize the acts of God in history.

While the rigid historical-critical method prevails on the continent, a few outstanding scholars recognize its limitations and insist that this purely scientific method is inadequate to understand the New Testament. Werner Kümmel, after surveying the history of New Testament science, comes to this conclusion: "When the historian takes seriously his task with reference to the New Testament, he must recognize that the New Testament demands of its reader something which he as a historian simply cannot give, namely, a judgment which is for every man the most important decision which is possible . . . . New Testament science in reality misses its task when the scholar feels that as a scholar he must shut his eyes to this claim."[4]

Leonhard Goppelt distinguishes between the historical-critical and the *heilsgeschichtliche* method. The latter interprets the New Testament as historical event accompanied by the apostolic witness as to the meaning of the Christ-event. While there is considerable variety in the apostolic witness, there is a basic unity of message which provides the basis for canonical Scripture. The bearer of the apostolic word is neither an exponent of a community faith nor an outstanding religious or theological personality; he is the bearer of a word which ever confronts him, and which is always more than the content of faith. Only in relationship to this interpreting word and in confession of it can the history of the early church be properly represented.[5]

More recently, Oscar Cullmann has expounded in detail this view of *Heilsgeschichte*. Revelation and redemption have occurred in historical events, culminating in the event of Jesus Christ. These redemptive events do not speak for themselves; they are always accompanied by a word of interpretation. The interpretation is not something extraneous to the events but

---

4 Werner Kümmel, *Das Neue Testament. Geschichte der Erforschung seiner Probleme* (Freiburg/München: Verlag Karl Alber, 1958), p. 520.

5 Leonhard Goppelt, *Christentum und Judentum* (Gütersloh: Bertelsmann Verlag, 1954), p. 13. The first half of this book has now been published in English under the title, *Jesus, Paul and Judaism* (New York: Nelson, 1964).

belongs itself to redemptive history. In the New Testament, the word of interpretation stems from eyewitnesses, particularly the apostles and prophets. The rise of the New Testament canon marks the final term of the entire preceding history of interpretation. This means that New Testament history must be interpreted theologically.[6]

The nature of this problem and defining the proper use of the historical-critical method have led to heated debate among the leaders of American biblical scholarship. On the one hand are scholars who continue to hold the older view and who deny that faith, which recognizes the acting of God in history, has any place in scientific criticism.[7] However, such scholars as F. V. Filson insist that the modern exegete can correctly interpret the Bible only when he accepts its claim about revelation and interprets the Bible in light of that revelation. The Bible can be rightly understood only by those who accept its basic message, and this requires the response of faith as well as a historical scientific methodology.[8] This "theological view of history" leads Filson to acknowledge the reality of the resurrection of Jesus.[9] In other words, the rigid rationalistic historicism which has usually characterized the historical-critical method is being modified by the soundness and effectiveness of the Bible's own witness to revelation.[10] This trend in contemporary biblical criticism ought to encourage evangelicals to more vigorous creative study in this area of biblical and historical study.

Second, we must acknowledge an enormous contribution to

---

[6] See Oscar Cullmann, *Heil als Geschichte* (Tübingen: Mohr, 1965).

[7] Cf. R. H. Pfeiffer, "Facts and Faith in Biblical History," *Journal of Biblical Literature,* 70 (1951), pp. 1-14.

[8] F. V. Filson, "Theological Exegesis," *Journal of Bible and Religion,* 16 (1948), pp. 212-15; "Modern Method in Studying Biblical History," *Journal of Biblical Literature,* 69 (1950), pp. 1-18.

[9] See *A New Testament History* (London: SCM, 1965), p. 163.

[10] The sterility of the old critical historicism has been frequently noted in quarters where it would hardly be expected. See Millar Burrows, *An Outline of Biblical Theology* (Philadelphia: Westminster, 1946), and Otto Baab, *The Theology of the Old Testament* (Nashville: Abingdon-Cokesbury, 1949).

our understanding both of the biblical world and the historical nature of the Bible itself. Critics have discovered ancient Greek manuscripts that give us a relatively early, accurate text in comparison to the poor late text that was used for the King James English translation. Critics have discovered that the language of the New Testament is not a tongue especially created to be the medium of revelation, but was basically the daily language of common people. Critics have discovered that the form of the Gospels is a new literary creation setting forth the Christian faith about Jesus of Nazareth. Critics have discovered many specific points of contact between the Bible and its historical environment. This ought to be expected; for if the gospel had no contact with its environment but only stood in contrast at every point, it could hardly have been understood and believed.

Research has also gathered a staggering accumulation of material which illustrates the New Testament. Strack and Billerbeck compiled four large volumes of illustrative materials from Jewish literature arranged in the form of a commentary; and Gerhard Kittel initiated an enormous theological dictionary on all of the important words of the New Testament, which provides extensive background for the use of these words both in the Jewish and Greek worlds. This work, begun in 1933, has already reached about 6000 pages and is still in process of being produced.[11] Archaeology has made amazing discoveries, bringing to light, for instance, the previously unknown existence of a library of a religious monastic colony living by the Dead Sea twenty-five miles from Jerusalem. This mass of historical information has, however, served not merely to illustrate points of contact between the New Testament message and its historical environment; it has also disclosed crucial points at which the biblical message is unique, standing in contrast with its environment.[12]

11 See above, p. 11.
12 See G. E. Wright, *The Old Testament Against its Environment,* and F. V. Filson, *The New Testament Against Its Environment* (Naperville, Ill: Allenson, 1952).

This ought to illustrate that biblical criticism *properly defined* is not an enemy of evangelical faith, but a necessary method of studying God's Word, which has been given to us in and through history. It is true that the historical-critical method, strictly interpreted, is based upon a rationalistic view of history, and is incapable of accepting the biblical witness of God's acts in history. However, some contemporary critics who were trained in this approach have recognized its sterility and unfruitfulness and have distinctly modified their assumptions of what could and could not have happened and reflect a much better understanding of the Bible's witness to its own revelatory character. There remain, unfortunately, those who cannot appreciate any but their own rationalistic understanding of biblical history and criticism; a fundamentalist mentality can be found in unexpected places.

It is a sad commentary on the state of evangelical scholarship that the names of few evangelical scholars appear among those men who have made a substantial contribution to our modern historical knowledge of biblical origins. This book does not pretend to be such a contribution; it does not attempt primarily to solve problems, nor even to defend the Bible as the Word of God, although this is assumed. Its purpose is to introduce the concerned student and layman to the study of the various types of biblical criticism, and to suggest areas in which evangelical scholarship ought to be more deeply concerned. Although our illustrations are drawn primarily from the New Testament, the basic principles of criticism are valid for the entire scope of biblical study.

CHAPTER III

Textual Criticism

ONE OF THE FIRST QUESTIONS THAT FACES THE STUDENT OF ANY ancient literature is the question of the original text. What did the original author really write? What words came from his pen? Is the text we use identical with its original form? This science of textual criticism has also been called "lower criticism" in contrast to "higher" or literary criticism; but neither term, "lower" or "higher" criticism, is really meaningful, for there is nothing "lower" or "higher" about either method of studying the Bible. It is better therefore to speak of textual criticism, designating thereby the study of the many variants in the text of the Bible and the effort to recover the original text.[1]

---

[1] The story of the text of the New Testament has often been told in excellent handbooks. See A. T. Robertson, *An Introduction to the Textual Criticism of the New Testament* (Nashville: Broadman, 1925); Frederic Kenyon, *Our Bible and the Ancient Manuscripts* (London: 1939); Frederic G. Kenyon, *Handbook to the Textual Criticism of the New Testament* (Grand Rapids: Eerdmans, 1951); Frederic G. Kenyon, *The Text of the Greek Bible* (London: Duckworth, 1949); Frederic G. Kenyon, *Recent Developments in the Textual Criticism of the Greek Bible* (London: Oxford, 1933); J. Harold Greenlee, *An Introduction to New Testament Criticism* (Grand Rapids: Eerdmans, 1964). However, one of the very best is also the most recent: Bruce M. Metzger, *The Text of the New Testament* (New York and London: Oxford, 1964). The author is deliberately following Prof. Metzger's excellent book as a guide with the hope that the interested reader of this brief summary will turn to Metzger's splendid study for further detailed information.

The turning point in the history of the text was the invention of printing by Johannes Gutenberg in 1450. Before that time all books had to be produced laboriously by hand. An "edition" of a given work could be produced by a group of scribes or copyists, who listened to a reader dictate from a "master" copy and wrote down what they heard. Even in our day of concern for precision, practically every book printed contains a few typographical errors not discovered by proofreaders. (The careful reader will doubtless discover a few undetected errors in the present work.) One consoling fact for a modern author is that every copy of a given edition will contain the same errors, and one will not need to check the text of every copy. It is obvious that, when each copy was written by hand by a different individual, as in antiquity, no two copies would be exactly alike; and in the multiplication of copies, errors inevitably would be multiplied.

Ancient books were very different in form from our modern volumes. The cheapest "paper" was a fragile material made by gluing together in opposite directions strips of pith cut from the heart of the papyrus reed. Since this material was not durable, most of the papyrus volumes of the New Testament have perished. In modern times, great finds of papyri, both biblical and secular, have been uncovered in the dry sands of Egypt, and we have some 75 Greek papyri of the New Testament, most of them containing only small fragments or at most a few pages.

A more durable material used in ancient books was a specially prepared form of leather, called parchment or vellum. This material was used in pre-Christian centuries and continued in use until the late middle ages when it was displaced by less expensive paper.

The usual form of ancient books was a scroll. These scrolls did not exceed about thirty-five feet in length, because anything longer became quite unwieldy. If an author wished to produce a larger work, he would use several rolls. The two longest books in the New Testament, Luke and Acts, would have filled an ordinary papyrus roll of 31-32 feet; and this practical consideration probably accounts for the fact that Luke issued his work in two volumes instead of one. The best-known illustration of these ancient scrolls is the collection of books found near the Dead Sea since 1947, called the Dead Sea Scrolls. This was the library of a Jewish sect contemporary with Jesus who formed a separatist community and not only copied the books of the Old Testament but also produced an extensive literature of its own. Most of these scrolls are of leather, not papyrus.

It should be obvious that such scrolls were awkward to handle, not only for the readers but also for the author or copyist. Around the turn of the second century, a new form of book was developed — the codex or leaf-form of book. A codex was formed by folding together sheets of papyrus and sewing them together. The codex form was also used for parchment books.

The writing on both scrolls and codices consisted of uniform columns two or three inches wide. The ancient style of Greek writing, called uncial, used in literary works was analogous to our capital letters, but the words were written together without breaks between them and virtually without punctuation. In the ninth century a new style was initiated consisting of smaller letters in a running hand, called minuscule. About this time punctuation began to be used. The modern division of the Bible into verses was not introduced until the sixteenth century.

Sometimes problems in the text arise around the question of word division. For instance, GODISNOWHERE can be interpreted, "God is now here," or "God is nowhere." So in I Timothy 3:16, we have the letters ΟΜΟΛΟΓΟΥΜΕΝΩΣ, which can be rendered as the single Greek word ὁμολογουμένως, "confessedly" (ASV), or as the two words ὁμολογοῦμεν ὡς, "we confess that (RSV) great indeed is the mystery of godliness." In such cases scholars have to make a judgment as to which rendering is the more likely.

We possess an almost overwhelming number of manuscripts of the New Testament.[2] In addition to the 75 papyri we have some 250 uncial manuscripts, that is, books produced between the fourth and ninth centuries; but many of them are incomplete, containing only part of the New Testament. In addition, we have more than 2600 minuscule manuscripts produced between the ninth and fifteenth centuries. In addition to these Greek manuscripts we possess the New Testament in other ancient languages, such as Latin, Syriac, Ethiopic, Coptic, Gothic, and Armenian. These translations are called versions. Often, problems in the Greek text can be illuminated by looking at these versions, for the text in these ancient translations may represent a good Greek text from which they were translated.

Of the versions, the Latin is the most interesting because of the rôle it has played in the Roman Catholic Church. The New Testament began to be translated into Latin as early as the end of the second century, and was widely used in North Africa and Europe during the third century. That it was often carelessly copied is proven not only by a study of the existing Old Latin texts but by the words of Augustine (d. 430) who complained, "no sooner did anyone gain possession of a Greek manuscript, and imagine himself to have any facility in both languages (however slight that might be), than he made bold to translate it." Jerome (d. 420) also complained that there were almost as many translations as there were Greek manuscripts; and this multiplication of poorly translated Latin texts is borne out by such facts as the existence of at least twenty-seven variant readings in the surviving Old Latin manuscripts of Luke 24:4-5.

So great was the obvious corruption of the Old Latin that in 382 A.D. Pope Damascus requested the most capable biblical scholar known to him, Jerome, to undertake a revision of the Latin Bible. This revision, known as the Vulgate, was based on

2 See B. M. Metzger, *op. cit.,* pp. 31ff.

the best Latin texts available, which were compared with some old Greek manuscripts. It is of interest to note that, under pressure of friends, Jerome added to his translation of the Old Testament certain later non-canonical books, although he recognized they were not a part of the canonical Scriptures. These "apocryphal" books gradually became a distinct collection, and finally in the sixteenth century were declared to be canonical by the Roman Church. A fine English translation of the Apocrypha is now available as a companion volume of the Revised Standard Version of the Bible.

The Vulgate itself in subsequent copying became badly corrupted. More than 8,000 manuscripts of the Vulgate have survived, and these are filled with divergent readings. The famous Council of Trent (1546) recognized the need for an authentic edition of the Latin Scriptures, which was prepared and published in 1592 by Pope Clement VIII, and the "Clementine" version has been the official Latin Bible of the Roman Church to the present day.

It would be interesting and informative to discuss the other ancient versions, but it is not necessary for our present purpose. The reader will find this story in Professor Metzger's excellent book.[3]

We must return to the story of the Greek New Testament. When Gutenberg invented printing, his first major publication was a magnificent edition of Jerome's Latin Vulgate, which is appropriately called the Gutenberg Bible. The first Greek New Testament to be printed (1516) was the work of the famous scholar Erasmus. Not being able to find a manuscript which contained the entire New Testament, Erasmus made use of several manuscripts for various parts of the New Testament; but he relied heavily upon two twelfth-century manuscripts which we now recognize as quite inferior. Lacking a complete copy of the book of Revelation, Erasmus himself translated the

---

[3] B. M. Metzger, *op. cit.*, pp. 79ff.

last six verses back into Greek from the Latin Vulgate. In other places in his work, Erasmus introduced into the Greek text material which he found in the Latin Vulgate but not in the Greek manuscripts. For instance, in Acts 9:6, he interpolated into his Greek text Paul's question, "And he trembling and astonished said, Lord, what wilt thou have me to do?" These words, which are found in the Latin, appear in no Greek manuscript known to us; they are easily explained as a harmonizing addition drawn from Acts 22:10.

The appearance of these words in the King James Version illustrates a very important fact which ought to be of great concern to modern readers of the English Bible. The so-called "Authorized Version," which was itself in fact a revision of previous English translations, was authorized by King James in 1611 and was based upon the Greek text of Erasmus. Since there were available to Erasmus only a half dozen late, inferior Greek manuscripts, the text which appears in the beloved Authorized or King James Version, for more than three centuries the Bible of the English-speaking world, is very inaccurate. As a matter of fact, Erasmus made limited use of his best manuscript, for he did not recognize its value. Most of the textual differences in the New Testament between the Authorized Version and the modern Revised Standard Version are not based upon the speculations of critics but upon three centuries of discovery of far superior Greek manuscripts.

Erasmus himself came under attack for omitting the theologically important trinitarian witness concerning "the Father, the Word, and the Holy Ghost: and these three are one. And there are three that bear witness in earth" (I John 5:7-8, AV). Erasmus defended himself by saying that these words, which appeared in the Latin Vulgate, could be found in no Greek manuscript known to him; but he promised to include them in his later editions if they could be found in a single Greek manuscript. When such a manuscript was produced, Erasmus kept his promise; and for this reason these words appear in the

King James Version. However, it now appears that the Greek manuscript in question was written in Oxford by a monk who took the words from the Latin Vulgate. In the thousands of Greek manuscripts now known, these words appear in only three, which date from the twelfth, fifteenth, and sixteenth centuries. In a dozen other passages in the Erasmian New Testament, readings occur which are supported by no known Greek witness.[4]

The story of the discovery and the utilization of new and more ancient manuscripts in the following centuries is a record of painstaking, incessant labor, but it is also marked with romantic episodes. One of the most tireless workers was Constantinus Tischendorf, who in 1869-72 published a two-volume Greek New Testament accompanied by a monumental apparatus indicating all of the variant readings known to scholars at that time. This work is now out of date, but it has not yet been superseded by a complete modern apparatus.

While still a young lecturer at the University of Leipzig, Tischendorf set out on a journey through the Near East in search of biblical manuscripts. At the foot of Mt. Sinai in the monastery of St. Catherine, he happened to see a waste basket filled with discarded papers in which he noted some leaves of parchment.[5] Examining them, Tischendorf found them to be leaves from a Greek translation of the Old Testament written in an early uncial script. He rescued forty-three leaves from the basket, and a monk informed him that two baskets full of similarly discarded leaves had been used to start the fire in the monastery. He was permitted to take the leaves back to Europe, where they can now be seen in the university library at Leipzig.

In 1859 Tischendorf returned to St. Catherine's monastery under the sponsorship of the czar of Russia. The day before he was to leave, he presented to the steward of the monastery a copy of the edition of the Septuagint (the Greek translation of the Old Testament) which he had recently published. There-

---

4 See Metzger, *op. cit.*, p. 101.
5 This oft-told story is related by Metzger, *op. cit.*, pp. 43ff.

upon, the steward remarked that he too had a copy of the Septuagint, and he produced from a closet in his cell a manuscript which proved to be the volume from which the forty-three leaves had been taken. Concealing his excitement, Tischendorf asked permission to examine the manuscript that evening. When his request was granted, Tischendorf retired to his room and stayed up all night studying this priceless discovery. To his delight, he found not only most of the Old Testament, but also the entire New Testament in excellent condition, and in addition two early Christian writings: the Epistle of Barnabas, previously known only in a poor Latin translation, and a large part of the Shepherd of Hermas, previously known only by title. (These two works are now readily accessible in the Loeb Classical Library in the collection known as the Apostolic Fathers.)

Tischendorf tried, without success, to buy the manuscript. He was, however, allowed to have access to it in a sister monastery in Cairo; and in two months Tischendorf and a number of assistants were able to transcribe in 110,000 lines of text the entire manuscript. Later, he persuaded the authorities at St. Catherine's that they could win the favor of the czar of Russia, the protector of the Greek church, if they would present the manuscript to him as a gift. Thus the priceless manuscript was made available to the world of scholarship. Photographic reproductions of it can be found today in most good theological libraries in America. After the Russian revolution, the U.S.S.R. sold the manuscript to the British Museum in London for $500,000 — a sale which attracted world-wide attention. This manuscript, called Codex Sinaiticus, dates from the early fourth century, and has proved to be one of the best texts we possess of the New Testament. If Erasmus had had access to it, our King James Bible would undoubtedly have a much more accurate text.

A manuscript of equal value is Codex Vaticanus, so called because it is housed in the Vatican Library at Rome. The existence of this manuscript was known already in 1475, when it was mentioned in the first catalog made of the resources of this great library. But the library authorities did not make it accessible to scholarly study until 1889-90, when a complete photostatic facsimile was published. Like Sinaiticus, Codex Vaticanus was produced in the fourth century; and some scholars have concluded that both of these Greek Bibles were among the fifty copies ordered by the emperor Constantine after his conversion. Codex Vaticanus contains both Testaments, with only three missing portions, and most of the Apocrypha. Its excellent text is very close to that of Codex Sinaiticus.

Sinaiticus and Vaticanus are only two of the some three thousand manuscripts now known and catalogued. Excellent as these two very ancient manuscripts are, the reader must not suppose that they preserve an errorless text. Marginal and interlinear readings in both these manuscripts indicate that they had been worked over by one or more correctors who noted places in the text which differed from the reading of the other manuscripts with which they worked.

Having indicated the wealth of materials available for producing a critical text of the New Testament, we shall now illustrate the kinds of errors which crept into the text as it descended from one copy to another. Some of these textual variations involve matters of theological importance; but the majority of them do not essentially affect the meaning of the Bible, and vast numbers of textual errors deal only with trivial differences. Such trivial variants can be important in tracing the history and relationship of manuscripts. Of all people, evangelicals who believe in an inspired Scripture should insist upon the greatest possible accuracy in the text. It is a strange anomaly that those who have most strongly emphasized the importance of verbal inspiration have often been the very ones who have most highly revered the English Bible which possesses a very inaccurate text.

Errors in copying the Greek text arose when the copyist did

not correctly read the text that lay before him. In I Timothy 3:16, the AV reads "God was manifest in the flesh," while the RSV reads, "He was manifest in the flesh." Some uncritical readers might attribute such a change to an alleged "lower theology" of the modern version; but the facts are simple. The earlier manuscripts read OC ("he who"), while many of the later manuscripts read $\overline{OC}$ (*theos* — "God"). The difference is only two small marks.

In II Peter 2:18 the AV reads, they "were clean [i.e., completely] escaped," while the RSV reads, they "have barely escaped." The difference in translation arises from confusing two very similar Greek words: ONTΩΣ (really) and OΛIΓΩΣ (scarcely). In this instance, the former reading is indeed found in Sinaiticus, and as a result found its way into most of the later minuscules and into the AV. But the latter reading is supported by the vast majority of best manuscripts.

A common type of error, made even by excellent stenographers, is the omission of one or more lines of text when two lines standing near each other end in the same word or words. Most modern typists use some sort of reading guide to keep the eye from straying as it returns to the script from the typewriter. This accidental omission often occurred in the copying of manuscripts. Codex Vaticanus, for example, has an impossible reading at John 17:15: "I do not pray that thou shouldst take them from the evil one." How could a scribe write such a senseless sentence? Easily:

> I do not pray that thou shouldst take them from the world, but that thou shouldst keep them from the evil one.

The scribe's eye moved unconsciously from the first line to the third without noticing the omission. In the same way, the entire verse, Luke 10:32, is lacking from Sinaiticus because both verses 31 and 32 end with the same verb: "passed by on the other side."

Errors arose from mistakes of the ear as well as the eye. Both the AV and the RSV read at Romans 5:1, "we have peace with God," while the margin of RSV gives an alternate reading, "Let us have peace with God." The difference in Greek is EXOMEN and EXΩMEN. The difference is only that of a long and short o, whose pronunciation was very similar. However, in the first person plural of the verb, this means the difference between an indicative ("we have") and a subjunctive of exhortation ("let us have"). In this instance, both readings are found in such good manuscripts that we cannot be certain which form Paul intended.

A similar variant reading of a single letter completely changes the meaning of a passage. Mark 7:19 speaks of food which cannot defile a man because it goes "into his stomach, and passes out into the drain, cleansing all foods." This English sentence is ambiguous; the Greek syntax is not. KAΘAPIZΩN, which is found in the best texts, is masculine, referring to Jesus. By this teaching Jesus "declared all foods clean" (RSV). In the later texts the word was written as a neuter, KAΘAPIZON, as though it referred to the foods which are cleansed from the body.

Our beloved Christmas story has the angels singing, "Glory to God in the highest, and on earth peace, good will toward men" (KJV, Luke 2:14). This translation rests on the late textual reading, EYΔOKIA. However, the better text reads EYΔKIAΣ, placing the word in the genitive case. The angels' song did not promise a vague peace to all men, but assured peace to those who are the objects of God's pleasure: "peace to men of (his) good will."

In Revelation 1:5, the AV reads, "washed us from our sins," while the RSV reads, "freed us from our sins." The difference in Greek is ΛOYΣANTI (washed) and ΛYΣANTI (freed); and the pronunciation of the diphthong OU and the vowel U could easily be confused. In this case, the former reading is found in the later texts and therefore appears in the AV, while the

RSV of necessity follows the best texts which have the second reading. Again, this change has nothing to do with the theological views of modern scholars; it is simply a matter of following the better text.

Other errors arose when a scribe made an unconscious slight alteration in the letters he wrote. The difference between the AV at Mark 14:65 "the servants did strike him with the palms of their hands," and the RSV, "the guards received him with blows," so far as the verb is concerned, is the difference between EBAΛON (struck) and EΛABON (received). The former reading is found only in the later inferior texts.

Errors of this sort sometimes resulted in a text which makes utter nonsense. One of our oldest Greek mansuscripts, Codex Bezae (fifth or sixth century), has a ridiculous reading at John 5:39. "You search the scriptures because you think that in them you have eternal life, and it is they that are sinning concerning me." This curious passage arose when a scribe read his master text carelessly. What he read was AIMAPTYPOYΣAI (they that bear witness); what he thought he saw and wrote was AMAPTANOYΣAI (they are sinning).[6]

Errors occurred when a copyist did not know how to handle the text he was copying. Sometimes a scribe would find words written in the margins of his source text. What should he do with these words? Sometimes such marginal readings were corrections which an earlier scribe had made of his own errors in copying the body of the text. Such marginal readings should be copied as part of the text. On other occasions, however, the marginal reading was not a correction of an error but a "gloss," i.e., a synonym for a hard word or an explanatory comment meant to illuminate the meaning of the text itself. In this case, the marginal reading should not be copied but omitted. But how could the copyist know which marginal readings were corrections and which were glosses? Since he was dealing with

6 Metzger, *op. cit.*, p. 193.

the Word of God, the safe course was to be conservative and not take the chance of leaving anything out of sacred Scripture. In this way, many marginal glosses have come into our later manuscripts.

Sometimes a gloss consisting of a single word can change the meaning of a text. For instance, in Matthew 5:22, according to most of the best texts, Jesus says, "Everyone who is angry with his brother shall be liable to judgment." This is a hard saying; who is there who never becomes angry? Is this not an unrealistically high standard? At an early date, a copyist explained what he thought was the meaning of this hard text by inserting into the margin the Greek word εἰκῇ, "without a cause." A later copyist simply transferred this word into the text, thinking it had been omitted; but in doing so, he changed the teaching of the passage. Jesus meant to say, "If murder is a sin, so is anger; for murder has its origin in an evil heart." He is not discussing unjustified anger but the heart of man which can harbor evil, hostility, anger against his fellows, which can in turn issue in murder. Perfect righteousness means a heart free from evil intent.

Sometimes such marginal additions involve entire verses. For instance, at John 5:3-4, the best manuscripts, some of the Old Latin manuscripts, and one of the earliest Syriac versions have the text as it is translated in the RSV, merely stating that many sick and infirm people lay near the pool of Bethzatha (four different spellings of this word are found in early manuscripts). At an early time, a copyist made a note in the margin explaining that these people were lying there waiting for the fulfillment of a popular tradition that an angel from time to time stirred the waters in the pool, giving them healing powers. A later scribe transferred this explanatory comment from the margin to the text; and it found its way into practically all late manuscripts.

The RSV appears to omit a very wonderful verse at Acts 8:37. After Philip preached the gospel from Isaiah 53 to the Ethiopian eunuch and he had asked for baptism, the familiar version reads, "And Philip said, If thou believest with all thine heart, thou mayest. And he answered and said, I believe that Jesus Christ is the Son of God." One might wonder how the translators of the RSV could have omitted such a logical and beautiful confession? The fact is that the RSV has not omitted anything, for the only early support for these words is in the Old Latin manuscripts. They first appear in Greek in a sixth- or seventh-century manuscript which contains the book of Acts in Greek and Latin. An earlier Greek and Latin manuscript known as Codex Bezae (fifth or sixth century) does not have these words; and they are wanting in all of the earliest Greek texts. This confession is therefore clearly no part of the original text of Acts, but was first written in the margin of a Latin translation and found its way later from the Latin into the Greek manuscripts.

A curious and apparently idiotic mistake appears in one fourteenth-century Greek manuscript of the Gospels. In Luke's genealogy of Jesus (3:23-38) an utter confusion of the names in this text results in nonsense. The scribe who wrote this manuscript obviously copied from an earlier document in which the genealogy of Jesus was arranged in two parallel columns of twenty-eight lines each, the first column ending at verse 33 and the second at verse 38. The scribe confused the two columns, and instead of copying them vertically in proper succession, he copied the genealogy as though the two columns were one, following the lines across both columns. As a result, almost everyone is made the son of the wrong father; and God is made the son of Aram; and Phares is listed as the source of the entire race.[7]

Thus, unintentional errors may result from faulty reading of a manuscript, faulty hearing on the part of scribe, unconscious lapses of the mind, or mistaken judgment, when a scribe believed a marginal notation to be part of the text. A second class of errors arose from intentional alterations made by a scribe who

---

7 See Metzger, *op. cit.*, p. 195.

felt that the text he was copying was in error and ought to be corrected. An interesting illustration of this is found in Codex Vaticanus, which has a distinctive reading at Hebrews 1:3. The prevailing text is, "bearing (ΦΕΡΩΝ) all things by the word of his power." The original copyist of Vaticanus had erroneously written: "manifesting (ΦΑΝΕΡΩΝ) all things. . . ." A later scribe, checking over this manuscript, noted the obvious error and corrected the variant reading to conform to the familiar text. A third, much later scribe, possibly of the thirteenth century, believing that manuscripts should stand as they are, changed the corrected text back to the original erroneous reading, and then indicated his displeasure by writing in the margin his judgment of the first corrector: "Fool and knave, can't you leave the reading alone and not alter it?"[8]

Such deliberate corrections are often quite inconsequential so far as the meaning is concerned and do not affect a translation into a different language. Rough Greek expressions may be made more smooth to produce a better style. Other deliberate changes are more noticeable. Some result from the harmonizing of parallel passages. Matthew and Luke have quite different versions of the Lord's Prayer, Luke's form being considerably shorter. Some manuscripts substitute Matthew's long version for Luke's short version. John 19:20 records that the superscription over the cross was written in Hebrew, Latin, and Greek; in our best manuscripts, no such comment appears at Luke 23:38 (see the RSV). However, early in the Latin translation, Luke was harmonized with John by the addition of this comment at 23:38. Thus the words found their way into most of the later Greek manuscripts and hence into the AV. Such deliberate harmonizing changes in the Gospels and in other parallel passages such as the three accounts of Saul's conversion are numerous.

Another type of deliberate harmonization is the change of quotations from the Old Testament to make them agree with

8 Metzger, *op. cit.*, pp. 195f.

their Old Testament form. For instance, a difference is found between the AV and the RSV at Matthew 15:8 in the citation from Isaiah 29:13. The RSV does not include a line which appears in the AV: "This people draweth nigh unto me with their mouth." None of the earlier manuscripts has this sentence. It was added by scribes at a later date who filled out the citation by comparing it with its source in Isaiah.

Other deliberate changes in text were made to round off the meaning of a passage. Matthew 9:13, for example, reads, "For I came not to call the righteous, but sinners." A relatively early copyist amplified this by adding the words, "unto repentance," which he found in Luke 5:32.

Another kind of smoothing addition is made with respect to the names of the deity. Galatians 6:17 reads, "I bear on my body the marks of Jesus." This seemed too abrupt to some scribes, and they amplified it to read, "the Lord Jesus," "the Lord Jesus Christ," or "our Lord Jesus Christ." The same tendency is found in many Christians today who do not like to refer to Jesus by that name alone, but feel that reverence requires that He always be spoken of as "the (our) Lord Jesus Christ."

A scribe would face a real problem when he found variant forms of a given passage in texts which he was copying. What should he do? Which reading should he choose? The safe solution would be to copy both; and this was often done. For instance, old manuscripts have two different endings for the Gospel of Luke. The two oldest, Alexandrinus and Sinaiticus, conclude with the words that the disciples "were continually in the temple blessing God." A different ending is found in the Old Latin translation and in the Greek-Latin Codex Bezae: they were "continually in the temple praising God." In practically all of our late manuscripts the two readings are combined to produce the conflated text which stands behind the AV, where the disciples are said to be both "praising and blessing God."

This illustrates adequately many of the kinds of errors which have arisen in the copying of Greek manuscripts. In most of the illustrations we have given, the solution to the textual problem is a relatively easy matter because the reasons for the errors are not difficult to detect. Through the developed science of textual criticism we have achieved a relatively accurate text of the New Testament. There remain, however, numerous readings where the weight of the divergent witnesses is so evenly balanced that it is impossible to decide with certainty which reading is to be preferred.

This may be illustrated by Acts 20:28. The reading "the church of God" (AV) is a bit stronger than "the church of the Lord" (RSV), and the former in fact appears in some of our critical editions of the New Testament. But the reading "the church of the Lord" is well attested, and the critic is faced with the question: could Paul speak about God purchasing the church with His own blood? This is not the biblical way of speaking, and the expression, "the church of God" cannot refer to the deity of Christ, but only to God the Father. The question of the correct reading is a matter for critical judgment, and one must deal in probabilities, because certainty cannot be reached.

Another interesting but difficult question is the ending of the Gospel of Mark. The problem is evident in the RSV handling of Mark 16. The text there ends at verse 8 with the words, "for they were afraid." In a footnote two endings are printed: the so-called "longer ending" which appears in the AV as verses 9-20; and a short ending which reads, "But they reported briefly to Peter and those with him all that they had been told. And after this, Jesus himself sent out by means of them, from east to west, the sacred and imperishable proclamation of eternal salvation." These two endings are printed in the RSV with the explanations: "Other texts and versions add as 16:9-20 the following passage," and "Other ancient authorities add after verse 8 the following."

This footnote fails, however, to indicate the complexity of the problem as it appears in the ancient texts. The fact is that at least *five* different endings exist for the Gospel of Mark. The "long ending," consisting of verses 9-20 came into the text of the AV because it appears in the great majority of the minuscules and in most of the later uncials, and was therefore a part of the prevailing text known in the seventeenth century. It can be traced back to a very early date, for it appears in a Syriac harmony of the Gospels made in the second century by Tatian. Its earliest appearance in the Greek sources is from the fifth century.

A second form of Mark ends at verse 8. As we have indicated earlier in this chapter, the two oldest and best Greek manuscripts, Sinaiticus and Vaticanus, dating from the fourth century, were not available to scholars until the nineteenth century. Both of these manuscripts lack this long ending, and conclude the Gospel abruptly at verse 8 with the words, "for they were afraid." This so-called "short ending" appears in many manuscripts of several ancient versions or translations; and some of the ancient church fathers state that verses 9-20 were lacking in Greek manuscripts known to them. Jerome says in one place, "Almost all the Greek copies do not have this concluding portion." Other late manuscripts which include the long ending contain a marginal comment which states that older Greek texts, known to the copyists of the later manuscripts, lack the long ending.

A third and altogether different ending to Mark is found first in an old Latin manuscript dating from the fourth or fifth century. The long ending (16:9-20) is lacking; but instead of ending abruptly at verse 8, this manuscript has the short addition which appears in the RSV footnote mentioned above, which smooths out with a brief summary statement the abruptness of the ending at verse 8. This short addition found its way into several late uncial manuscripts of the seventh, eighth, and ninth centuries, and is found in a few minuscule manuscripts and in several other ancient versions.

A fourth form of Mark 16 appears in a few manuscripts which have both endings; the short addition after verse 8, followed by the long ending of verses 9-20.

A fifth ending was known to Jerome. We have already noted that Jerome was familiar with many Greek manuscripts which ended at verse 8. However, Jerome also knew the long ending in a novel form, which included an enlargement of Mark 16:14:

> And they excused themselves, saying, 'This age of lawlessness is under Satan, who does not allow the truth and power of God to prevail over the unclean things of the spirits. Therefore reveal thy righteousness now' — thus they spoke to Christ; and Christ replied to them, 'The turn of years for Satan's power has been fulfilled, but other terrible things draw near. And for those who have sinned I was delivered over to death, that they may return to the truth and sin no more; that they may inherit the spiritual and incorruptible glory of righteousness which is in heaven.'[9]

In 1906 a new manuscript of the four Gospels was discovered dating from the fourth or fifth century, known as Codex Washingtoniensis, which was found to contain this long variant known to Jerome.

We have deliberately taken time to spell out the problem of the ending of Mark in rather full outline to acquaint the lay reader with the complexity of textual criticism. What does the scholar do when he finds such bewildering diversity? Does he simply "play it safe," and, lest he omit part of the Word of God, reconstruct a text that includes all variants? This procedure was often followed by ancient scribes. Obviously, this would add to the Word of God passages which do not belong to it. It is quite clear, for instance, that in the ending of Mark, the short addition and the amplification at 16:14 have such weak textual support that they cannot be seriously considered as authentic. They are obviously additions by later scribes.

This leaves the scholar with two questions: can the longer ending (16:9-20) be authentic? If not, how is the abrupt ending at 16:8 to be explained?

In answering the first question, the textual evidence is supported by literary considerations. Although the long text has

9 See Metzger, *op. cit.*, p. 57.

ancient attestation and, even if inauthentic, was clearly produced at an early date, our two oldest and best manuscripts
omit it. This textual consideration is reinforced by the literary
fact that in these twelve verses, seventeen words are used which
either appear nowhere else in Mark's Gospel or are used very
differently from the way Mark used them. In other words, the
long ending is written in a non-Markan style. These facts, together with other considerations, have led most modern scholars
to the conclusion that the long ending which appears in the
AV is not authentic, but was produced by a copyist at an early
date to smooth up the abrupt ending at 16:8.

This conclusion raises a further problem: does Mark 16:8 preserve the original ending of Mark, or was the Gospel mutilated
at an early date so that the last column of Mark's original text
has been lost? A good number of modern scholars have defended
the view that nothing has been lost, that Mark exercised great
literary subtlety in ending his Gospel with the words, "for they
were afraid." This, however, seems rather incredible. Professor
Metzger appears to be right in his conclusion that the note of
fear would not have been regarded as an appropriate conclusion
to an account of the Evangel or Good News.[10] It is credible that
very soon after its production, the fragile papyrus scroll in which
Mark was written was damaged so that the last few inches were
torn off, and all subsequent editions of Mark reflect this loss.
This conclusion finds some further plausibility in the fact that
Mark was not a widely used Gospel in the ancient church because practically everything appearing in Mark was included
in Matthew, and the longer Gospel therefore overshadowed
the shorter.

This discussion points to an important fact in textual criticism.
Although it can be called a science because it deals with objective
facts and well-established principles, textual criticism cannot
be considered a pure objective science, for at many points, as in
the problem of the ending of Mark, judgments must be made,
hypotheses formulated, and various possibilities debated.

[10] *Op. cit.*, p. 228.

Before concluding this chapter, we must make a brief survey of the history and the principles involved in the establishing of a trustworthy text. A completely uncritical exercise of textual criticism would be a simple numerical approach. The best text would be one which is supported by the largest number of manuscripts and versions. The poorest is that supported by the fewest texts. A moment's reflection will show this to be unsafe. If, for instance, ten manuscripts are copies of a single parent manuscript, then an error appearing in the parent will appear ten times in the ten copies; and these ten authorities are equal to a single authority, not to ten.

This points to an all-important principle which upon reflection seems to be almost self-evident, but which did not emerge in the history of textual criticism until the eighteenth century and was not put on a firm scholarly basis until the last half of the nineteenth century. This is the principle that manuscripts should be classified into groups or families of texts. This classification into families is based upon agreement of a group of manuscripts in a large number of variant readings; and for this purpose the variants which are most trivial as far as the meaning of the text is concerned can be important in establishing family relationships. For instance, if a group of four manuscripts can be shown to embody fifty or a hundred common readings, however unimportant, which are found nowhere else, it can be safely concluded that these variants stem from a common source. Perhaps all four manuscripts were copied from a single parent manuscript which is no longer extant; perhaps three of them are copies of the fourth; perhaps the four are copied from two related parent manuscripts. Several possibilities exist, but the sharing of a group of common variants reflects some kind of family relationship.

The vast majority of the approximately five thousand Greek manuscripts, especially the late uncials and most of the minuscules, share a large group of variant readings *which are not found in our oldest sources.* This discovery led two of the greatest modern textual critics, B. F. Westcott and F. J. A. Hort, in the late nineteenth century to establish the cornerstone of all modern scientific textual criticism: that the vast bulk of our manuscripts embody a type of text which came into existence in the fourth century A.D. and which combines the readings of earlier texts. The editors of this fourth-century text, wishing to produce a smooth, easy, and complete text, combined readings which they found in the earlier texts known to them. This so-called "Syrian text" was distributed throughout the Byzantine Empire, and was reproduced in practically all later manuscripts. This fact was not known in the sixteenth and seventeenth centuries when the first Greek New Testaments were printed and the King James Version translated. As we have already seen, the so-called *Textus Receptus* or "received text" which was embodied in the first printed New Testaments and which underlies the AV translation was based on a few late minuscules, which we now know represent the latest and poorest textual family — the Syrian or Byzantine family.

Westcott and Hort further established what earlier scholars had been suspecting, namely, that back of the fourth-century Syrian text several earlier families or groups of texts could be detected. Westcott and Hort suggested three such families. Since that time, their conclusions have been further refined, but they have not been overturned. They found in Codex Bezae (fifth century), in the manuscripts of the Old Latin translation, in the Old Syriac translation of the Gospels, and in the Old Latin fathers such as Marcion, Irenaeus, Tertullian, and Cyprian a group of common readings which arose in the western part of the Empire in Italy and North Africa. This Westcott and Hort styled the "Western" text. In another group of manuscripts, supported by the Egyptian (Coptic) translations and the Alexandrian fathers such as Clement, Origen, Dionysius and Cyril, Westcott and Hort found a text containing a group of variants which reflected an effort to produce a polished, smooth, grammatical text. This attempt would be natural in this Alexandrian center of learning and culture, and Westcott and Hort designated this "revised" text by the term "Alexandrian."

The most trustworthy text Westcott and Hort found in the two oldest fourth-century manuscripts, Sinaiticus and Vaticanus, which agreed with each other at numerous places against all other texts. Believing this text to be the most free from the process of refinement, corruption, and mixture which pervaded the later texts, they called it the "Neutral" text, intending by this term to indicate a text family that had avoided the corruptions and refinements that came into both the Western and the Alexandrian texts. Westcott and Hort further postulated that the Alexandrian and the Neutral text types were descendants of a common ancestor, but that the Neutral text (Sinaiticus and Vaticanus) preserved it quite accurately, while the Alexandrian text was both polished and influenced to some degree by the Western text.

This basic solution to the textual problem has been almost universally accepted. Westcott and Hort published their work in 1881, and both the English Revised Version (1881-1885) and the American Standard Version (1901) are based upon their work. Research in the last eighty years has resulted in further identification of smaller families, particularly within the so-called Western text; but the basic Westcott and Hort solution still stands.

In concluding this survey of textual criticism, we must raise a question which has seldom been faced by evangelicals who believe in the plenary inspiration of Scripture, especially by those who revere the old King James Version. Does not a belief in an inspired original text demand the preservation of an infallible text? Does not the existence of numerous errors in the text of the English New Testament which one is using mean that this text is really not the infallible Word of God? What is the effect of these numerous admitted errors upon the concept of an infallible Scripture? Is the recognition of the Bible as the inspired Word of God impossible if there are admitted errors in the text of Scripture? Evangelical believers must face this question seriously and honestly.

To formulate the question in sharp perspective, let us be reminded that the form of the Word of God used and loved by millions of believers for three-and-a-half centuries has been the King James or Authorized Version of 1611, which was based upon the *Textus Receptus* of the first printed New Testaments, which in turn was based upon the Syrian (Byzantine) family represented by the numerical majority of the late manuscripts. Compared to the text established by more recent scholarship, the *Textus Receptus* is a poor text and is studded with thousands of textual errors, which are embodied in the beloved Authorized Version. This is not a matter of faith or theology; it is a simple, objective fact.

This may be illustrated by one of the pioneers in the development of textual criticism, J. A. Bengel (d. 1752).[11] When Bengel was a very devout university student, his faith in the plenary inspiration of the Bible was disturbed by the existence of some 30,000 variants in the text of the most recent edition of the Greek New Testament — that of John Mill, published in 1707. He determined to devote himself to the study of the transmission of the text, and he procured all the editions, manuscripts, and early translations then available. His study led him to formulate the principle that has since prevailed in textual criticism, namely, that the text must be studied not in terms of numerical readings, but in terms of family groupings. He was thus the first to distinguish between the family represented by the mass of late manuscripts and the families represented by Alexandrian and Latin (Western) texts. His lifelong study led him to the important conclusion that the thousands of textual variants did not bring into question any article of evangelical doctrine.

This raises again the important question: what do we mean when we say that the Bible is itself the Word of God? This is a question often misunderstood and misrepresented. Belief in

11 See Metzger, *op. cit.*, pp. 112f.

verbal inspiration, that is, the work of the Holy Spirit that inspired not only the authors of Scripture or their ideas but also
the expression of these ideas, does not lead to the conclusion
that the Bible is a magical book and that the words are an end
in themselves. Otherwise we should worship the Bible instead
of the God of the Bible and fall into the idolatry of bibliolatry.
Words have value only as they express ideas and convey truth,
and the gospel is not mere words but the good news about what
God has done for man's salvation. Belief that the Bible itself is
the Word of God does not lead to a worship of the Bible or to a
mechanical or mathematical view of the words of the Bible. It
does mean that God in revealing Himself has used the vehicle
of human words, first spoken by the prophets and apostles, then
written; and that the Bible is the one vehicle by which man can
know both God and redemptive truth about God and His
saving purpose for mankind. The statement that the Bible itself
is the Word of God means that we have complete confidence in
the truthfulness of the Bible, in its message, in what it teaches
about God, man, redemption, and human destiny. In other
words, it is the message of the Bible that is important. Our
survey of textual criticism proves that it is a simple fact that
the possession of a trustworthy message does not depend upon
the establishment of the exact words of Scripture at every point.
As Bengel concluded, the variants in the text do not affect any
essentials of evangelical truth.

We may express this fact in a different way. In spite of the
poor text of the *Textus Receptus,* we must recognize that the
Textus Receptus and the King James Version are indeed the
Word of God. In this inspired work, men can hear God speak;
they can meet God and be brought into saving fellowship with
Him. For three-and-a-half centuries, the King James Version,
with its thousands of errors in the text, has been the only Word
of God known by millions of believers. Because of its dignity,
beauty, and familiarity, many Christians even today cannot
feel at home with any other translation, and they read the

Authorized Version as though the very English words have been given immediately by God.

This fact, however, ought not to lead us to ignore the defects of the outdated text underlying the familiar King James. The careful student who is concerned about accuracy and exactness may continue to read the old version for devotional purposes; but for careful Bible study, he will certainly want to use a modern translation which is based upon the best text modern scholarship can establish.

Here is an area where critical scholarship has made a solid and permanent contribution which involves only to a minimal degree the problem of theological presuppositions. It is a seldom disputed fact that critical science has to all intents and purposes recovered the original text of the New Testament. There remain indeed numerous debatable and debated readings; but if one compares our four contemporary critical texts of the New Testament, edited by E. Nestle (1963), G. D. Kilpatrick (1958), R. V. G. Tasker (1964), and Kurt Aland—M. Black—B. M. Metzger—A. Wikgren (1966), he will find them to be in substantial agreement. In practically all of the illustrations cited in this chapter to illustrate textual criticism, the problems presented are soluble, and we have a reliable text.

The entire question of the text illustrates the larger problem of the relationship of biblical criticism to the Word of God. Textual criticism does not imply that the scholar is sitting in judgment on the Word of God or is criticizing it; he is merely using critical and scientific skills to establish what the text is. This exercise of criticism is absolutely indispensable, for it is quite clear that although God inspired the authors of the Bible to produce a divinely superintended record, he has committed the reproduction and the preservation of the text to the vagaries of human history; and the establishment of a trustworthy text is the labor of a scientific scholarship. This is not to suggest that God's providential hand does not rest upon all of human history; but it does insist that the Holy Spirit was active in the production of the biblical documents in a way different from their preservation and recovery. It also means that in the search for a good text, piety and devotion can never take the place of knowledge and scholarly judgment. One does not solve a problem of divergent textual readings by prayer or by the inner illumination of the Holy Spirit, but only by an extensive knowledge and skill in the science of textual criticism.

In conclusion, our survey of the most basic kind of criticism — that of establishing an accurate text — illustrates the necessity of criticism as a whole and its rôle in the study of the Bible. Criticism is necessary because God has revealed Himself and given to men His revealing Word through historical personages, events, and processes; and criticism deals with the questions that are inevitably raised by the historical dimension of God's Word. Admittedly, we would be in a much simpler and easier situation if the Bible had been given magically; but this was not God's way.

The role of biblical criticism is not to criticize the Word of God but to understand it. Textual criticism does not ask: Is the Word of God true? It asks: What is the text of the Word of God? How far can we re-establish the exact words through which God revealed Himself? And Christians of every tradition owe it to a critical scientific scholarship that we have in the last century achieved a trustworthy text.

CHAPTER IV

Linguistic Criticism

WE HAVE SEEN IN THE PRECEDING CHAPTER THAT AFTER GOD GAVE
His Word to men, He committed the text to the course of history; and it is the task of a scientific textual criticism to establish a trustworthy text. In this chapter we must illustrate that
the very meaning of the words of the New Testament can be
established only by a scientific linguistic criticism. The character
of the language of revelation is the most eloquent proof that
the Word of God has been given to us in the words of men.
A scientific understanding of the nature of New Testament
Greek has been achieved only in the twentieth century, and it
carries important implications both for our understanding of
the nature of revelation and for our attitude toward the English
Bible.

The double identity of the Bible as both the Word of God
and the words of man is an amazing phenomenon; and it is
easy to forget or to overlook one aspect or the other. Ultimately
revelation is a supernatural act of God. It is not merely identical with human reflection and speculation, which can be universally experienced. To be sure, human reflection and thought

are not set aside; revelation employs the media of human thought, reflection, and experience. Revelation, however, only occurred when God was acting among and speaking to men in a distinctive way to disclose His redemptive purpose. Revelation is not a human attainment nor a product of human knowledge and wisdom; it is God's Word spoken to men, and then expressed in the words of men.

Paul makes this quite clear. "For since, in the wisdom of God, the world did not know God through wisdom, it pleased God through the folly of the *kerygma* to save those that believe" (I Cor. 1:21). Human reason, speculation, philosophy, have produced many false ideas as well as true insights about God. These cannot, however, bring the lost sinner into a saving relationship with God. This can be accomplished only through the *kerygma* — the gospel, the proclamation of what God has done to bring man to Himself. If God had not acted, man would be forever lost. But God did act; God did speak; and God can be savingly known through the *kerygma*.

This word is translated as "preaching" in the AV, and the meaning would seem to be that the saving revelation occurs through the foolishness of the act of preaching, that is, the foolishness of proclaiming the gospel through a human voice. This is, however, misleading, for the word *kerygma* can also mean the message itself instead of the act of proclamation. The RSV translates correctly: "through the folly of *what we preach*," that is, the gospel, the Word of God formulated in the words of men.

This Word is not a human discovery, a product of human wisdom. Indeed, human wisdom sees it as foolishness, for the most degrading form of death, execution as a common criminal on a Roman gibbet, is claimed to be the highest revelation of both the justice and the love of God. Paul asserts that the highest point of revelation occurred in the deepest pit of human tragedy — a crucifixion. Here God was incarnate; here God was both sharing and bearing the tragedy, the sin, the death of men; and in this divine act in history, He was bringing men salvation.

This illustrates further the fundamental character of revelation as a deed-word complex, which we have discussed in an earlier chapter. Revelation occurred in deeds, and the redemptive meaning of these deeds is disclosed by the accompanying prophetic word. The death of Jesus is a "bare" historical fact, which today is scarcely ever denied by the most radical historical critics. Historically, it was an ugly, brutal, bloody, revolting spectacle. At that precise moment *it was not understood to be an act of revelation.* On the contrary Jesus' death on the cross meant to the disciples a denial of everything they had thought He might mean. One of His disciples said, "We *had hoped* that he was the one to redeem Israel" (Luke 24:21); but His death shattered every hope. The Word of God asserts that the death of Jesus on the cross is the supreme proof that God is indeed a God of love. "But God shows his love for us in that while we were yet sinners Christ died for us" (Rom. 5:8). "In this is love, not that we loved God but that he loved us and sent his Son to be the expiation for our sins" (I John 4:10). But this revelation of God's love on the cross was not a self-evident fact. The disciples who watched Jesus die did not throw themselves to the ground in thankfulness crying out, "I never knew how much God loved me." The Gospels do record that at least two men saw something unusual at the cross; a fellow victim prayed to Him, and one of the soldiers recognized a more than human dimension. But in both instances, the impressive thing was Jesus' bearing and conduct, not the fact of His dying. The cross itself was naked tragedy to all who beheld it.

The event of the cross, accompanied by words interpreting its meaning, is revelation. Apart from words explaining the meaning of the deed, revelation is not complete. This is not to deny that revelation and redemption occurred objectively, "out there," on the cross; but the cross was not known and could not be known for what it really was — the event of revelation of God's love and redemption — without the words of men which were the Word of God. These divinely given words, first uttered by the resurrected Jesus Himself (Luke 24:25-27) and later expounded by the apostles, do not read into the cross something which is not there; they merely serve to reveal what was really happening, what God was actually doing in Jesus' death.

This is the *kerygma* through which God speaks to men: the divinely inspired interpretation of a divine redemptive event, set forth in human words, which are at the same time the Word of God. This is Paul's meaning of the expression "the folly of what we preach": the recital of redeeming events in history and the divinely given explanation of the meaning of these events, expressed in human words.

This brings us to the main subject of this chapter. What is the historical nature of the words in which the revealing event is recorded and the revealing interpretation expressed? Are these words in their linguistic and literary character divine words, or are they human words which are historically conditioned and which must therefore be interpreted grammatically and historically?

The language of the New Testament is Greek. The Renaissance revived the study of the ancient classical Greek, and it did not require an expert to observe that the Greek of the New Testament was not identical with the language used in the Golden Age of Athens in the fifth and fourth centuries before Christ. Distinct differences were observed in vocabulary, in syntax and style, as well as in the form of words. Furthermore, the New Testament idiom differed from such contemporary first-century authors as Diodorus, Strabo, Plutarch, and even the Jewish authors Philo and Josephus. We know now that as men of culture, they were attempting to conform to the ancient classical literary idiom.

The distinctive idiom of the New Testament led many scholars from the seventeenth century to describe it as due to the influence of Hebrew. Other devout scholars argued that the Greek of the New Testament was the special idiom of revelation, "the language of the Holy Ghost."

A basic solution to this critical debate was provided in the decades following 1890 when, for the first time, archaeology brought to light masses of papyri containing first-century non-literary Greek. Most literary works of antiquity, including the Bible, have been preserved on a kind of leather-parchment or vellum, which is quite durable. Papyrus, the ancient equivalent of paper, is very fragile, and could only survive in an arid climate. On one occasion, workmen were seeking archaeological treasures in the dry sands of Egypt, but found only the pre-served forms of stuffed crocodiles. In disgust, one workman vigorously struck one of the crocodiles with his tool, only to find inside of it rolls of papyrus inscribed with Greek writing. Subsequent systematic research and accidental discovery have brought to light masses of documents containing all sorts of records written by ordinary common people in the daily lan-guage of the home, street, and market place. The nature of these writings covers the entire range of ancient social life: official documents such as deeds, business contracts, tax receipts; personal records such as correspondence, love notes, invitations; religious formulations such as magical incantations, expressions of gratitude to the gods, and the like. In these records the col-loquial language comes to light as it was spoken and written by everyday people who made no pretence to preserve an ancient classical literary idiom.

It was soon recognized that this colloquial, non-literary, *koine,* or common language, provided the basic idiom for the New Tes-tament. For the first time biblical scholars attained a scientific understanding of the true nature of the language of the New Testament. One of the first scholars to recognize the linguistic significance of the new papyrus finds was Adolf Deissmann, professor at Heidelberg and Berlin. Although liberal in his theology, Deissmann, like many other liberal scholars, has placed the entire world of biblical scholarship in his debt; and this debt must be acknowledged. In his famous *Bible Studies* (1901) and the even more famous *Light from the Ancient East* (1910), he provided a mass of accurate scientific philological and literary illustrations which place the New Testament idiom in its true historical perspective as the non-literary idiom of common people.

This very fact has profound implications for the philosophy of Bible translations. The English-speaking Christian world, and especially the evangelicals in it, has been largely unconscious of the fact that in its constant, sometimes passionate, insistence upon the sanctity of an ancient "authorized" version, it has ignored the historical fact that the Holy Spirit chose as the language of the New Testament revelation the colloquial language of everyday people, not an ancient classical ideal. The modern insistence upon the supremacy of the King James Version of 1611 represents a reversal of the action of the Holy Spirit by insisting that for us the best idiom for the Word of God is not the modern living colloquial idiom but the ancient classical language of Shakespeare. We should not overlook the fact that the idiom of Shakespeare and particularly of the Authorized Version of the Bible have made an indelible impression upon the history of English letters and language. Its familiar verses have been memorized by generations of adults and children. We cannot reverse the stream of history. The King James Version will never cease to be loved and used. But it remains a fact that this reverence for an idiom which is over three centuries old actually goes against the work of the Holy Spirit, who chose the living, colloquial Greek as the language of revelation. The example of the Holy Spirit would encourage us to insist that every generation have its own, up-to-date translation of the Bible in a contemporary living idiom. The King James Version, to put it bluntly, embalms an idiom long dead. We do not address one another today with such forms as "Thou," "Thee," "Thine"; we never say in current idiom, "Thou oughtest," "the wind bloweth where it listeth," "whosoever readeth," "ye wot not." We love this idiom because we have so long associated it with the Christian faith. Hardly a Christian cannot quote John 3:16 in the King James Version. But this does not change the fact that the King James idiom is no longer a living tongue.

More important, the outdated idiom of the King James Version often obscures the meaning of the Word of God, for ancient words have changed their meaning in the twentieth century. Too often we assume that we understand a text merely because we are familiar with it. Why are we to pray in a "closet" (Matt. 6:6) rather than in the study, den, or bedroom? How can I get a "mote" in my eye (Matt. 6:4)? What does it mean to "strain at a gnat" (Matt. 23:24)? What are "bowels and mercies" (Phil. 2:1)? Why did Paul have to "take up the carriages" in traveling to Jerusalem, instead of riding in them (Acts 21:15)? Why was a "compass" needed between Syracuse and Rhegium (Acts 28:13)? How can the living "prevent" the dead at the return of the Lord (I Thess. 4:15)? These are only a few of the many passages where a change in the meaning of the language has actually made the ancient version meaningless. If we accepted the example set by the Holy Spirit in choosing the non-literary, contemporary idiom to be the Word of God, we would insist on a modern translation which renders the ancient Greek as accurately as possible in idiomatic twentieth-century language.

The critical study of New Testament language has enlightened our understanding of the meaning of the Word of God at innumerable points. Again, it should be honestly admitted that it has been largely the work of critical scholarship, often quite liberal in its theological perspective, which has opened up to us a more exact meaning of the Word of God. A few illustrations will suffice.

The Greek word δοκίμιον occurs only twice in the New Testament. In James 1:3 the AV reads, "knowing this, that the *trying* (δοκίμιον) of your faith worketh patience." Christians are not to be discouraged when they meet various kinds of temptations, for such experiences which provide a testing or trial of one's faith produce character in the form of "patience" or "steadfastness." This is clear. In spite of this, can one say that the trial (δοκίμιον) of one's faith is a thing more precious than gold (I Pet. 1:7, AV)? The King James Version can be understood to mean that it is one's faith that is much more precious than gold; but in the Greek this is impossible: it is the *trial* of faith that is called precious. But this is difficult to square with Christian experience. Jesus Himself taught us to pray that we be not led into temptation (Matt. 6:13); but if such temptations provided a precious testing of faith, we ought to desire them.

Modern philological criticism based on the papyrus discoveries has found that δοκίμιον can have a second meaning: not the act of trial, but the result of trial: the genuineness, the approvedness of the thing tried. It is the possession of a faith which has been tested and found true which is a precious thing. The trial itself is painful, grievous, tragic. However, God can use pain, suffering, temptation to bring good; and the believer who has been through the fires of temptation and to whom it has been proved that he has a strong faith that can stand fearful testings has something precious which the Christian who has lived a sheltered, protected, easy life does not have.

New light is shed upon many other words showing that much of the New Testament idiom is simply an adaptation of the current colloquial meaning. Jesus said of the religious leaders of His day who basked in the adulating recognition of men, "They have their reward" (Matt. 6:2, 5, 16). The significance of this statement is now illustrated by the discovery that the verb was used in daily commercial idiom of a debt that was paid in full. When this is applied to people whose religious devotions are more a matter of ostentation than of private relationship to God, it means that such persons have been "paid in full" in the coin of human recognition. They have nothing more to expect from God.

On several occasions, Paul speaks of the gift of the Holy Spirit as an ἀρραβών (II Cor. 1:22; 5:5; Eph. 1:14). This is translated "earnest" in the King James Version and "guarantee" in the Revised Standard Version. It is doubtful whether "earnest" conveys any accurate meaning to most lay readers of the Bible, even though the word remains today in the seldom used expression, "earnest money." Frequently examples of the term are found in business transactions preserved in the secular papyri to designate a "down payment." In the ancient world, as is often true today, a purchase was bound by an initial payment of part of the total amount agreed upon — a down payment. The down payment or earnest money served a twofold purpose: it provided the seller with an actual amount of cash although not the full amount; and it was a token of the good faith of the buyer, thus providing a tangible promise or guarantee of the subsequent payment of the full purchase price.

When Paul applies this figure to the present gift of the Holy Spirit, he places Christian experience in an eschatological context. That is to say, he relates what the believer now experiences in a sinful world and a weak physical body to the perfect eternal life of the age to come. The RSV is only partly right when it renders ἀρραβών by the English "guarantee." The present gift of the Holy Spirit is a guarantee of the future consummation of salvation at the second coming of Christ; but it is far more than guarantee. It is also a "down payment," a real participation, an actual experience of the eternal life of the age to come.

This is clear in Ephesians 1:14, which is obscure in the AV: "which is the earnest of our inheritance until the redemption of the purchased possession." The RSV clears up the difficulty considerably: "which is the guarantee of our inheritance until we acquire possession of it." The man in Christ has a future inheritance — resurrection, immortality, eternal life, to be received at the second coming of Christ. However, the Christian life is more than a mere promise of a future salvation; it includes a "down payment," in the form of the gift of the indwelling Holy Spirit, of what is to be received in the future.

This understanding places the whole Christian life in a new light. Christians are to display in a sinful, fallen world a bit of what the future life is to be like, because they have already been given a down payment of that future life. It is indeed only a partial payment; and for this reason the believer, like others, remains a weak, mortal sinner. But he must be different, for he has something which other men have not experienced. God has imparted to him through the Holy Spirit an actual preliminary participation in the future inheritance, until at the consummation of redemption, the people of God will be taken to be His possession.

Another important word whose meaning had been known but whose theological usage is vividly illustrated from its secular background is παρουσία (parousia). This is one of the words used to describe the return of our Lord. Its basic meaning is simply "presence." In Philippians 2:12, Paul exhorts his readers to obedience whether in his presence (παρουσία) or in his absence (ἀπουσία). The word is also used in a more limited sense of the coming or arrival of a traveler. Paul speaks of the encouragement he found on one occasion by the "coming (παρουσία) of Titus" whose arrival brought Paul good news about the Corinthian church (II Cor. 7:6).

This meaning might suffice to illustrate the "coming" of the Lord (Matt. 24:3, 27; I Cor. 15:23; I Thess. 2:19; 3:13; 4:15). However, the use of the word in the Hellenistic papyri now shows that the term had come to carry a semi-technical significance, designating official visits of persons of high rank, especially of kings and emperors visiting a province. On the occasion of such visits, special taxes were often levied upon the people of the favored city or district to defray the official's expenses and to provide a costly crown for the official. Against this secular background, the New Testament usage gains new significance, for Paul writes that the Lord will make His appearance for the purpose of bestowing crowns upon those who love and serve Him (I Thess. 2:19; II Tim. 4:8).

These illustrations suffice to show how the modern discovery of the true historical character of first-century common Greek throws new light on the meanings of New Testament words. We have chosen as illustrations words which carry important theological and devotional meanings. A scientific philology must apply this kind of critical historical study to every New Testament word. Until a few years ago, the best Greek lexicon or dictionary in English was the work of J. H. Thayer, published in 1886. Thayer listed some 767 "New Testament" words, which appeared to belong to the distinctive "biblical Greek." However, Deissmann's researches in the papyri reduced this list to 50, and the list continues to shrink. Frequently, all that is involved is the spelling of a word, or a slight change in form; but all such minutiae must be studied exhaustively. In addition to the words themselves, all details of variation in word inflections, grammar, and syntax must be analyzed.

Having illustrated the modern discovery that New Testament Greek is at its base the common vernacular language of the first century, we have only told part of the story; for the event of revealing, redemptive history in Jesus Christ did not take place in Alexandria or Ephesus or Rome, but in Palestine, where Aramaic was the common language of the people. Furthermore, the revelatory event in Christ stands in a line of direct continuity with the redemptive history recorded in the Old Testament. As such it is the fulfilment of the promises made to the prophets, and it affects the character and idiom of the New Testament language. The language of the New Testament cannot be completely understood and explained in terms of Hellenistic Greek; it also embodies a large Semitic element, both from the vernacular Aramaic which Jesus used, and from the Greek translation of the Old Testament (the Septuagint)·

Palestine in the first century of our era contained a mixture of Jewish and Greek culture.[1] Although Aramaic was the native tongue of Palestinian Jews, Greek was widely spoken. Jesus must have discoursed with the procurator Pilate in Greek (John 18:33ff.), but several indications in the Gospels prove that he commonly taught in Aramaic. Several Aramaic expressions have been preserved and merely transliterated into Greek. To the prostrate form of Jairus' daughter Jesus said, "Talitha cumi";

[1] A delightfully written, non-technical book which discusses such problems is G. A. Williamson, *The World of Josephus* (London: Secker and Warburg, 1964).

and Mark translates these Aramaic words, "Little girl, I say to you, arise" (Mark 5:41). To a deaf man, Jesus said, "Ephphatha," which is Aramaic for "Be opened" (Mark 7:34). The most striking instance of Aramaic is Jesus' cry from the cross: "Eloi, Eloi, lama sabachthani" (Mark 15:34). These are words taken from Psalm 22, which begins, "My God, my God, why hast thou forsaken me?" Jesus did not formulate His prayer in the Hebrew of the Psalm, but in its Aramaic equivalent.

The fact that Jesus' Aramaic teachings have been translated into Greek in our Gospels raises a difficult historical problem. To what extent can we recover this process of translation? When and how did it occur? Were Jesus' teachings first written down in Aramaic and these written documents later translated into Greek? Many scholars have thought so, at least in the case of one of the Evangelists' sources for the teachings of Jesus.[2] Or were the teachings of Jesus rendered into Greek while they were still preserved in oral form before written documents were produced?[3] We know that Jesus' Aramaic teachings were translated into Greek, but we cannot recover the process of translation with any certainty.

The important question is, to what extent did the translation from Aramaic to Greek affect the form of the teachings? Torrey built his theory of original Aramaic Gospels largely on the basis of alleged mistranslations in our Greek Gospels of the supposed Aramaic originals; but Torrey's erudition is more impressive than the soundness of his illustrations. One of the basic problems in any such theory is that we possess little contemporary Aramaic literature by which we can reconstruct the vernacular Aramaic idiom of Jesus' contemporaries; and specialists in Aramaic studies debate the question of which extant Aramaic litera-

---

2 See, for example, M. Black, *An Aramaic Approach to the Gospels and Acts* (Oxford: Clarendon, 1954), pp. 270ff., for the view that the source Q (German, *Quelle*, source) was written in Aramaic. (For further explanation of Q see chapter V.) One famous scholar, C. C. Torrey, promoted the theory that all four Gospels were first written in Aramaic and later translated into Greek; but this theory has found little support.

3 For the question of oral Gospel tradition, see chapter VI.

ture best represents the spoken tongue of early first-century Palestine.

In some places, the Aramaic background explains the differing form of the Greek in the Synoptic Gospels. To give only one illustration: Luke 6:20 reads, "Blessed are you poor," whereas Matthew 5:3 has, "Blessed are the poor in spirit."[4] Back of both expressions lies the Aramaic (and Hebrew) *anawim* (Ps. 37:11; 40:17; 70:5). The *anawim* are the poor, devout people, seen in contrast to the rich and mighty. The mighty vaunt themselves, flaunting God and oppressing the poor, while the poor find their one source of strength and help in God. This concept thus combines the idea of a humble social status and a humble dependence on God. Luke emphasizes the former aspect, Matthew the latter.

The Old Testament background for New Testament language can be seen most vividly in the Greek transliteration of Hebrew terms which are not part of the Greek vocabulary. Such words are ἀλληλουιά (hallelujah) meaning "praise Yahweh," βάτος (bath) designating a Hebrew liquid measure of about 8-9 gallons (Luke 16:6); μάννα (manna); πάσχα, the Passover; σάββατον (Sabbath); σατανᾶς (Satan); ὡσαννά (hosanna), a Hebrew term of prayer and praise.

The New Testament word γέεννα (*gehenna*) designating the state of final condemnation (Matt. 5:22, 29; 10:28; 18:9; 23:33) results from the transliteration of the Hebrew *ge hinnom,* "valley of Hinnom," a ravine south of Jerusalem where debris was burned and human sacrifices offered (II Kings 23:10; II Chron. 28:3; Jer. 7:32). Ἀββά (*Abba*) (Mark 14:36; Rom. 8:15; Gal. 4:6) is an Aramaic form meaning "father." A contemporary Aramaic scholar, Joachim Jeremias, has emphasized that this was the most intimate term that children used to their parents, something like the English "Papa" or "Daddy." It was such an intimate term that Jewish rabbis would not use it of God; but this intimacy stands at the heart of the Christian gospel.

Another Aramaic term, *Amen,* is impossible to translate into

4 See below, p. 120.

English. Jesus often used this word to give authority to His words: "Amen, I say to you."[5] This is rendered "verily" by the AV and "truly" by the RSV, but neither word conveys the force of the Semitic term. "Amen" is used in the Old Testament as a solemn formula to confirm the validity of an oath (Num. 5:22; Deut. 27:15-26), to give assent to an announcement (I Kings 1: 36), or as a doxology. Jesus' use of the word to introduce a statement has no parallel in rabbinic usage; He employed it as the equivalent of an oath, paralleling the Old Testament expression, "As I live, saith the Lord."

An understanding of the Semitic background of the New Testament and of Old Testament influence upon it is not only important for the comprehension of those Semitic words which have been transliterated into Greek. Many Greek words have a different meaning in a Hebrew context than they would in a Greek context. For example, the Greek word χριστός (Christ) is simply the adjective derived from the verb χρίω "to anoint." In the Greek wor'.l the designation χριστός carried no theological or religious significance, neither was it a proper name. However, the equivalent term in Judaism, *hamashiah*, represented a title, "the Anointed One," "the Messiah," "the Christ." In Hebrew life kings (I Sam. 9:16), priests (Ex. 28:41), and prophets (I Kings 19:16) were anointed with oil to ordain them to their divinely appointed office; and in New Testament times the term *meshiah* specifically designated the promised Davidic King who would deliver God's people and establish His Kingdom.[6] Gentiles unacquainted with the Old Testament were undoubtedly puzzled by the use of the term, a confusion which is reflected by the Roman historian Suetonius, who referred to the founder of Christianity by the name *Chrestus,* "the kind one," rather than *Christos.*[7]

In the Gospels χριστός is used almost always as a title for

---

[5] Thirty times in Matthew, 13 in Mark, 6 in Luke, 25 in John. Luke often substitutes other expressions, such as "truly."

[6] This usage appears most vividly in the pseudepigraphical Psalms of Solomon 17 and 18, where it appears in its Greek form.

[7] *Life of Claudius* 25.

Jesus, not as a proper name; He is not Jesus Christ, but Jesus, the Christ (or Messiah).[8] Only in the epistles of Paul, which reflect the Christian language of the Gentile churches, does χριστός become a common proper name for Jesus; but even Paul sometimes uses the word as a Jewish messianic title (e.g., Rom. 9:5).

The Greek word ψυχή (*psyche*), usually translated "soul," provides another example of a New Testament Greek word which must be understood in the light of a Hebrew context. For the Greek ψυχή could be conceived of as something other than the body, that is, the essence of the true self. This is the ordinary understanding of the English word soul. But the basic New Testament meaning of ψυχή is like the Hebrew *nephesh*, that is, the animating principle, the life of the body. Sometimes ψυχή designates no more than physical life. It is in this sense that not only men but animals have life (ψυχή). Revelation 8:9 reflects this Old Testament idiom when it speaks of creatures in the sea which have ψυχή (AV translates, "creatures which . . had life"; RSV, "living creatures"). When Jesus warned against worry about one's bodily life, the Greek word is *psyche* (Matt. 6:25). The word is also used in Jesus' declaration that it was His mission to give His *psyche* a ransom for many (Mark 10:45). The word in this context probably designates simply Jesus' purpose to give His life as a sacrificial offering.

Because ψυχή is the life of man, it can be used by metonymy of man himself. The literal translation of Romans 2:9 in the AV, "every soul of man," means idiomatically, every person. "Let every soul be subject to the higher powers" (Rom. 13:1) carries no psychological implication; "every soul" means simply everyone. The baptism of "three thousand souls" on the day of Pentecost (Acts 2:41) is a literal translation which has been carried into the English expression "a community of a thousand souls."

As the life principle, ψυχή is also used to designate the inner

8 E.g., Matt. 1:17; 2:4; 11:2; 22:42; 23:10; 24:5, in the RSV. In all these references AV mistranslates the term as though it were a proper name.

life of man. It can be grieved (Matt. 26:38), troubled (John 12:27), pained (Luke 2:35), exalted (Luke 1:46), full of love (I Thess. 2:8, see AV; Matt. 22:37), full of righteousness (II Pet. 2:8). God is even spoken of in anthropomorphic terms as having a soul (Matt. 12:18; Heb. 10:38). Men are said to be "of one heart and soul" (Acts 4:32), in other words, in harmony with one another.

The New Testament also uses ψυχή to designate the center of life which transcends bodily existence and is therefore the special object of salvation (James 1:21; 5:20; I Pet. 1:9; 2:25; Heb. 10:39) and of Christian nurture (II Cor. 12:15; Heb. 13:17). The chief concern of man should not be the soundness of his body but the preservation of his soul (Matt. 10:28; Mark 8:35, 36;[9] 9:43ff.). Thus ψυχή can be used of the souls of the dead (Rev. 6:9; 20:4; see Heb. 12:23: the "spirits of just men" are made perfect after death).

These illustrations are sufficient to show that ψυχή is a very complex and difficult term, with meanings ranging all the way from the animating principle of all earthly creatures (life) to the essential self which can exist apart from the body and which is the object of salvation (soul). But this philological fact raises an even more difficult question. Do we see in this word two different concepts: a Hebrew meaning (life) and a Greek meaning (soul)? If so, can the history of the development from one meaning to the other be traced? This philological question points to a larger historical and theological problem which stands at the center of biblical theology, the problem of the Hebrew and Greek views of man.

Hebrew and Greek thought involve two different psychologies and two different world views. In late Greek thought, man is a duality of soul or spirit imprisoned in a body. This duality reflects a cosmic dualism: the visible, transitory world, and

9 The RSV renders ψυχή by "life," but the saving of one's ψυχή certainly refers to the preservation of one's true life after the death of the body. The contrast here is between gaining "the whole world," that is, this world, including its intellectual, emotional, and physical satisfactions, and forfeiting one's true life at the second coming of Christ (v. 38).

the invisible, eternal world. The realm of the material is the sphere of darkness and sin; the realm of the spirit is light and life. As body, man is involved in the changing, sinful, decaying world; but his true life is found in the pure realm of the soul or spirit which is imprisoned in the material dying body. His true destiny is to escape the evil realm of the material and to take his flight from the visible to the invisible world of eternal reality. Bodily life is thus a spurious life that is ultimately unreal; true life is the life of the soul or spirit which must be delivered from entanglement in evil matter.

The Old Testament reflects no such dualism. The material world, including man in his bodily existence, is not in itself the realm of evil, but is God's good creation (Gen. 1:25, 31). The ultimate destiny of man in God's redemptive purpose is not to escape from sinful, bodily, earthly existence to attain to a glorious disembodied existence with God in heaven; it is bodily, social life on a redeemed earth. This redemptive goal resounds repeatedly in the prophets (cf. Amos 9:13ff.; Isa. 2:1-4), and ultimately demands the resurrection of the body (Isa. 25:8; 26: 19; Dan. 12:2).

The New Testament writers share this Old Testament perspective. Sin does not reside in the world of matter — in man's having a body, but in his will. Therefore, the goal of salvation includes the redemption of the body (I Cor. 15; Heb. 11:35) and the entire created order as well (Rom. 8:21) in a new redeemed earth (II Pet. 3:13). The New Testament never conceives of the salvation of the soul apart from the body. Redemption always means the salvation of the entire man: body, soul, and spirit (I Thess. 5:23). The Bible is of course aware of the eternal realm of God and pictures Jesus as coming down from above (John 3:31; 8:23), but the goal of redemption is not an escape from earthly existence to a distant heaven, nor a flight to a different eternal order of existence; it is a new world in the Age to Come (John 12:25; Mark 10:23-30; Heb. 2:5; 6:5).

If the New Testament shares the basic psychology and world

view of the Old Testament, a difficult question is raised. How did the New Testament come to use ψυχή in a way which seems closer to Greek thought than to that of the Old Testament? Is this due to Greek influence in the development of biblical language and concepts? There is no *a priori* reason why divine revelation might not make use of elements of truth from the world of Greek thought.

However, the word ψυχή is used in the New Testament according to the theology of the Old Testament, not according to the cosmic dualism of the Greeks. This is proved by three facts. The first has been already expounded: New Testament redemption is never the salvation of the soul *from* the body or salvation of the soul *without* the body, but salvation of the soul *with* the body.

Secondly, the New Testament clearly goes beyond the Old Testament in conceiving of the soul as capable of existing after the death of the body, but this separation of the soul from the body is never pictured as the final goal of salvation. It is rather a state of temporary blessedness in anticipation of the resurrection of the body.

Thirdly, the Old Testament itself contains intimations of this "intermediate" state. It does not picture man as an immortal soul divinely implanted in a mortal body. Death is therefore not the flight of the immortal soul to be with God; it is the descent of man to *sheol,* the realm of the dead. Usually, it is not the souls of men who dwell in *sheol*; it is men themselves, pictured as "shades" (*rephaim*), who are pale, weak replicas of men on earth. This Old Testament picture of the shades of men in *sheol* after death reflects the view that death is not the end of human existence, but it is not life; for life means conscious fellowship with God and the enjoyment of God's blessings in both the spiritual and material spheres; and this can be fully experienced only in bodily existence.

Therefore, although it is only occasionally affirmed, eternal life demands the resurrection of the body (Dan. 12:2). There are, however, a few indications in the Old Testament that the shadowy existence in *sheol* is not God's last word for His people.

"For thou dost not give me (*naphshi* — "my *nephesh*") up to *sheol,* or let thy godly one see the pit. Thou dost show me the path of life; in thy presence there is fullness of joy, in thy right hand are pleasures forevermore" (Ps. 16:11). Here shines forth the assurance that God will lead the soul of the righteous man from the lifeless realm of the dead — *sheol* — into His own presence where he will enjoy life, that is, fellowship with God. Again, "God will ransom my soul from the power of *sheol,* for he will receive me" (Ps. 49:15. See also Ps. 73:24).

In such sayings, God disclosed to the Old Testament saints the truth which is clarified in the New Testament: that the death of the righteous means "to depart and be with Christ" (Phil. 1:23), or to be "away from the body and at home with the Lord" (II Cor. 5:8). However, this intermediate state is not the goal of redemption. Man's final destiny is always the resurrection of the body that "what is mortal may be swallowed up by life" (II Cor. 5:4) at the coming of the Lord Jesus, "who will change our lowly bodies to be like his glorious body" (Phil. 3:20) when we "attain the resurrection from the dead" (Phil. 3:11).

This rather lengthy discussion of the New Testament use of ψυχή illustrates the kind of question which confronts the serious student in the study of New Testament words. The gospel, which is the record and the interpretation of God's redemptive acts in Christ, has its background in the Old Testament; but it is expressed in first-century Greek, in a literature written largely for a Greek audience, using terms well known in popular Greek philosophical thought. Therefore the careful student must take both the Old Testament and the Greek backgrounds into consideration.

What we have said about the history of the word ψυχή applies also to the other important words used to designate man: πνεῦμα (spirit), σάρξ (flesh), and σῶμα (body). We cannot illustrate this principle further at this point; but each of these terms must be examined closely against both the Hebrew and Greek backgrounds. When this is done, the New Testament psychology will be found to be much more Hebraic than Greek, although the words used are Greek. However, evangelical scholars need to give far more attention than they have to the question of the Greek element in New Testament theological idiom.

Another vivid illustration of a Greek word filled with a Hebrew meaning is the word for God's covenant with men: διαθήκη. The Greek world used this word to indicate a last will and testament, by which a man disposed of his possessions at death. The use of this word in Hebrews 9:16 is a deliberate play on the word διαθήκη, when the author moves from the idea of covenant to that of a will or testament.

However, the usual meaning of διαθήκη in the New Testament appears infrequently in classical times. It comes directly from the Old Testament *berith* or covenant, which God made with His people (Gen. 15:18; 17:7, 10; Ex. 19:15, *passim*). Sometimes *berith* is translated "contract"; but this English word generally suggests a bilateral agreement made between equals, whereas *berith* presupposes no relationship of equality between the partners. Often it is an agreement imposed by a superior on an inferior (see Josh. 9:6ff.; I Kings 20:34; I Sam. 11:1ff.). Or it may refer to an agreement in which the second party is not compelled to enter into covenant but it is to his interest to do so.[10]

The Greek had a better term to express a bilateral agreement between equals: συνθήκη. It appears that the translators of the Septuagint (the Greek Old Testament), fully aware of the difference between *berith* and συνθήκη, deliberately chose to use the word διαθήκη, thus filling it with a significance not common in the Greek world: an agreement initiated by a sovereign God and offered to man. The covenant was thus divine and unconditional in its inception, offering to men blessings which they had not sought nor merited. The covenant required a response on the part of man, which was fulfilled in the ritual of circumcision (Gen. 16:14), and in keeping "the

10 See G. von Rad, *Old Testament Theology* (New York: Harper and Row, 1962), I, 129.

way of the Lord by doing righteousness and justice" (Gen. 18:19). This covenant was renewed at the time of Exodus from Egypt (Ex. 19:5, 6; 34:10) and sealed with sacrificial blood (Ex. 24:8); and the covenant became the center of Israel's relation to God. The prophets look forward to a day when the covenant will assume the proportions of a "new covenant," when God will do a new work in the hearts of His people which will enable them to enjoy a new and intimate fellowship with Him (Jer. 31:31-34).

This is the background for the New Testament concept of the new covenant based on Jesus' death (I Cor. 11:25), represented in the Last Supper (Mark 14:24), which fulfills the prophecy of Jeremiah 31 (Heb. 8:8ff.). The Christian faith is grounded upon the divine initiative in offering to men through the death of Jesus Christ a redemption which they did not seek and did not merit. The new covenant is, however, conditional as the old one was. It requires a human response: faith in Him who made the covenant in His blood (Heb. 10:16-22).

We have selected several important words to illustrate that the New Testament language has as its base the vernacular first-century Greek, but that the idiom expounding the New Testament revelation must be studied against its Semitic background since it is employed in expounding the meaning of a redemptive history moving from the revelation in the Old Testament to the redemptive event in Jesus Christ.

This dual background of the New Testament idiom points out the task that must be carried out by an adequate linguistic criticism. The shades of meaning of New Testament words must be examined in terms of their secular Greek background, their religious usage in the Septuagint, and their revelatory meaning in the New Testament. It was this monumental task that Gerhard Kittel, beginning in 1933, set out to accomplish in his unrivaled *Theologisches Wörterbuch zum Neuen Testament*. Already over 6000 pages have appeared, and the work still goes on.[11] The usual format of this work is to study a word or a

11 See footnote, p. 11.

word-complex in the Old Testament, then to analyze the equivalent words in the Greek language, then to trace the equivalent terms in Judaism (in the Septuagint, in Jewish writing, both Hellenistic and Palestinian, usually including the rabbinic literature), and finally to conclude with an analysis of the word or words in the New Testament. So extensive are these studies that some fourteen of them have been translated and published as separate little books, each about a hundred pages long. All of this work has been done by German "critics" who are the modern representatives of the historical-critical method, and the serious student of any theological conviction cannot ignore such massive scholarship.

We would conclude this chapter by pointing out that such linguistic study must be carried out in a scientific spirit. Of course, there remain many unsolved problems and innumerable debatable questions. But questions of historical philology are not answered by the depth of a student's religious devotion nor by his theological convictions. On the contrary, the positions taken by systematic theology must rest upon the findings of scientific philology.

An example of this can be found in a technical problem that would go unnoticed by the average layman: that raised by the Greek word ἱλαστήριον in Romans 3:25. The AV translates the word as "propitiation"; the RSV has "expiation." Both of these words have lost their distinctive meanings to masses of Bible readers, and some systematic theologians say it really doesn't matter. If sin is expiated, God is propitiated. But in the technical study of the biblical language, two entirely distinct concepts are involved which are not interdependent in the judgment of most New Testament scholars. The translation "expiation" means that sin is covered; the translation "propitiation" means that, in some sense, God's wrath is appeased or satisfied. In short, the translation of the AV involves a different theology from that of the RSV.

The problem is not solved by accusing the translators of the RSV of having a "lower" theology, for their conclusions rest upon technical linguistic study, not simply upon theological persuasion. In 1935, C. H. Dodd, perhaps the leading British New Testament scholar, published a book entitled *The Bible and the Greeks* which contained a detailed study both of the Greek and the Hebrew words which stand behind ἱλαστήριον in Romans 3:25. He concluded that the idea of sacrifice as a means of propitiating God's wrath is indeed the meaning of the verb ἱλάσκομαι in pagan Greek literature. However, he insisted that this idea is not biblical and is found in neither the Old nor the New Testament. Dodd argued that the Hebrew idea of *kipper* and the Septuagint-New Testament idea of ἱλάσκομαι mean only that sin is covered, not that God is propitiated.

This conclusion would, of course, modify the traditional orthodox interpretation of the meaning of the death of Christ. An easy but futile way of answering Dodd would be to accuse him of liberal theology and ignore his findings. But scholarship must deal with the evidences that a scholar presents, not with judgments of his motivation.

This has been done by a very able evangelical scholar, Leon Morris. In an outstanding study,[12] he covers the same ground as Dodd and uses the same methodology, but comes to different conclusions. He argues that Dodd overlooked certain important considerations which point in a different direction. Morris demonstrates that the idea of propitiation is present in the word group. We are not to think that Christ by His death so appeased the wrath of God that the divine wrath was converted to love. On the contrary, it is God's love itself which effected the satisfaction of His own wrath in the death of His Son (II Cor. 5:19-21). Morris' conclusions, like Dodd's, are achieved only by painstaking linguistic study. There is no short cut in dealing with such problems.

Other vital questions remain debatable. We may conclude by a single illustration. The most exalted Christological passage in the writings of Paul is Philippians 2:5-11; but the

---

12 *The Apostolic Preaching of the Cross* (Grand Rapids: Eerdmans, 1955).

language involves exquisite exegetical difficulties. There appears to be a play on two words: μορφή in verses 6 and 7, and σχῆμα in verse 8. Christ pre-existed in the form (μορφή) of God; he assumed the form (μορφή) of a servant, that is, of a man, and thus was found in the "fashion" (AV; Greek σχῆμα) of a man. What is the μορφή of God? What is the μορφή of man? An easy answer would be that the μορφή of God means essential deity; the μορφή of man means essential humanity; the σχῆμα of man means the outward form in which humanity is embodied. This may well be Paul's meaning, and it is supported by the technical meaning of these words in Greek philosophy, which used μορφή to designate inner essence and σχῆμα to designate outward form. However, it is a clearly established philological fact that Hellenistic Greek often lost the fine distinctions found in classical Greek, and many scholars feel that this distinction claims too much.

Whatever the μορφή of God is, how is this μορφή of God related to "equality" with God? Are they identical? Is μορφή equal to deity? Or is it the manifestation of deity — the divine glory? Did the pre-existent Christ possess the μορφή of God but not equality with God?

An even more difficult question is the meaning of "robbery" (AV) or "grasped" (RSV) in verse 6. Without going into details, we can only say that the Greek word ἁρπαγμόν can mean either the seizing of a thing, or a thing held onto. Both the AV and RSV are ambiguous: "Robbery" can mean "an act of robbery" — the seizing of something; or it can mean "the object of robbery" — the holding on to something which has been seized. "A thing to be grasped" can mean either that it is seized, or that it is held onto. The Greek word ἁρπαγμόν can have both meanings, but the sense of the passage is quite different depending on which meaning is chosen.

If the word is rendered, "the seizing of something," the meaning is that the pre-existent Christ did not possess equality with God; but although He existed in the form of God, He did not consider equality with God something to be seized as something rightfully His. Instead of seizing equality with God, He emptied Himself by becoming a man.

If the word is rendered "something to be held onto," the meaning is quite different. The pre-existent Christ possessed both the μορφή of God and equality with God; but He did not consider this equality with God something to be held forcibly, but surrendered it up in becoming a man. It is not our purpose at this point to solve the problem, but only to suggest that the best scholarship is required in the study of such delicate problems.

A final question: What is the meaning of ἐκένωσεν (v. 7)? The AV renders it, "he made himself of no reputation," while the RSV settles for the straightforward meaning of the word, "he emptied himself." Here again is a delicate exegetical problem: does the verb imply some object? Of what did Christ empty Himself? Of the μορφή of God? Of equality with God? The "boldest" exegetes have maintained that Christ in His incarnation emptied Himself of His deity, or at least of the exercise of it; and there has arisen around this word a whole "kenotic" school of theology. However, the word in the text has no object; perhaps it needs none. Perhaps the idea is that He did not empty Himself *of* anything; He emptied *Himself* in an act of humiliation. This appears to be the meaning intended in the AV translation: "he made himself of no reputation."

Thus far in our discussion of Philippians 2 we have only suggested the kind of questions which the serious interpreter must ask. At this point, it is possible only to suggest one interpretation of the passage without proof; adequate support would require an additional chapter and a very technical discussion. The passage may be paraphrased thus: "Who, though he shared deity, did not count equality with God the Father a thing to be seized, as was his right. On the contrary, he poured himself out by taking upon him human nature, being born in the likeness of men. Being found in human form, he humbled himself and became obedient unto death, even death on a cross. Therefore God has highly exalted him and bestowed on him the name which is above every name — Lord; that at the name of Jesus every knee should bow . . . and every tongue confess that Jesus Christ is Lord. . . ." Thus, because of His self-outpouring and obedience to death, God bestowed on Him the equality which He would not seize.

It is the author's hope that lay readers may not be too badly confused at this point. It is necessary to reinforce the point that Bible study is a very serious and exacting business; and there are many points where dogmatism can never be a substitute for careful exegetical study. But for every baffling problem which remains, the student will find innumerable passages where modern critical philology has shed much light upon the meaning of New Testament language. It is our hope that this chapter has adequately demonstrated this fact.

He who would preach and teach the Word of God, who would proclaim, "Thus saith the Lord," must study the Word of God in the words of ancient men. When he has learned to do this, he will find his ministry vastly richer, deeper, and more accurate.

CHAPTER V

Literary Criticism

As we noted in the last chapter, the term "lower criticism" is often used to designate what is properly called "textual criticism." "Higher criticism" is a phrase often used to refer to a critical literary analysis of the biblical books themselves, a science which is better termed "literary criticism." The names "lower" and "higher" criticism are actually quite meaningless, for there is nothing "lower" or "higher" about the two types of criticism. Furthermore, the pejorative phrase "The critics say . . ." is usually intended to designate a radical type of criticism which is destructive to the integrity of the biblical records. "The critics" are viewed as men who treat the Bible only as the words of men, and not as the Word of God. We are here urging a broader definition of criticism.

When any student recognizes that the Bible is the words of men, and tries therefore to answer questions about authorship, date, provenance or place of writing, sources, and unity, he is engaging in biblical criticism, even while he recognizes that the Bible is the Word of God.

At this point an important question for those who recognize

the Bible to be inspired by the Holy Spirit is this: to what extent did the Holy Spirit work through ordinary historical means, and to what extent were these ordinary methods transcended? If the biblical writers were truly inspired of God, must we not understand that they received and wrote their message by direct conscious impartation from the Holy Spirit?

A correct criticism must take into consideration the fact that the biblical authors were often conscious of their inspiration. The prophets did not speak out of their own merely human volition, but were moved by the Holy Spirit to speak the Word of God (II Pet. 1:21; see Jer. 1:9; Isa. 6:8ff.; Ezek. 3:1ff.). Paul, speaking and writing as a prophet and apostle, conscious of apostolic motivation, speaks with an authority that would be intolerable dogmatism and vain arrogance if his thinking were governed by nothing more than the human factor. He invokes a curse on those who disagree with his understanding of the gospel (Gal. 1:8). He appears intolerant of any disobedience to the instructions contained in his letters to the churches (II Thess. 3:14). He insists that his letters be read in the gatherings of the churches for public worship (I Thess. 5:27; Col. 4:16), even as the Old Testament was read. The reason for Paul's authoritative words is his consciousness that he has been appointed as a prophet and apostle to a divine office to speak the Word of God (Col. 1:25), to be the vehicle of the divine revelation of God's redemptive purpose (Eph. 3:4f.). For this reason Peter already recognizes Paul's writings as standing on a level with the Old Testament (II Pet. 3:15f.).

However, this quality of inspiration which produces a normative, authoritative Scripture did not set aside the media of ordinary historical experience and communication. The psychological nature of inspiration is, by its very character, impossible to understand and to explain. Sometimes the prophets were conscious of the Word of God as an outward power gripping their souls and compelling them to speak (Jer. 20:9). Ezekiel likens his reception of God's Word to God's giving him a scroll, which he ate, and so was commissioned to speak to Israel the Word of God (Ezek. 2:8-3:3).

But while the prophets were inspired, they were historical persons addressing themselves to historical situations using the media of communication current in their times. Perhaps the most vivid illustration of this communication of revelation through historical media in the New Testament is the book of Revelation. John is very conscious of being the vehicle of revelations; he writes in a book what God has given him to see in vision and commissioned him to write (Rev. 1:11, 19; 2:1ff.; 14:13; 19:9; 21:5). He therefore pronounces a blessing on those who hear and keep the words of his prophecy (Rev. 1:3) and invokes a curse on those who reject it (Rev. 22:18-19). Yet no book in the Bible is more human than the Revelation, for the Greek is studded with clumsy constructions and grammatical errors. Some of these appear to be deliberate, such as the expression in 1:4, "Grace to you and peace from the one being and the he was and the coming one." Even this clumsy translation (this is not a typographical error) does not reflect fully the difficulty of the Greek, for the entire construction is governed by the preposition "from" and ought to be in the genitive case, but is written in the nominative.

In many other places, the rules of correct grammar are violated. Prepositions are followed by incorrect cases; words in the same construction disagree in form; the article is used where it ought not to be. Criticism must attempt to explain this defective Greek, and numerous theories have been propounded. Some critics have argued that the style of Revelation is throughout a deliberate creation of the author for effect. Others argue that the author simply did not know the Greek language and wrote with a "barbaric" style. Perhaps he was a Jew who thought and wrote in Aramaic and had as yet imperfectly mastered Greek. Possibly the book was originally written in Hebrew and translated imperfectly into Greek. Perhaps the author was so enraptured by the visions he had seen that in ecstasy he simply ignored the rules of correct composition.

This imperfect character of the Greek of Revelation raises a real difficulty in accepting the strong ancient tradition that the John who wrote the Revelation is also the author of the Fourth Gospel. The Greek of the Gospel is simple but correct, smooth and flowing; the Greek of Revelation is incorrect, rough, and uneven. Could the same man have written two books with so different a style? This is a legitimate and unavoidable critical question. It is of course important to note that neither the Gospel nor Revelation claims to have been written by the Apostle John. The author of the Gospel is not named, and the author of the Revelation designates himself as John the prophet, not the apostle (Rev. 1:1, 3). Many critics have concluded that the two books are so different both in style and content that they could not have been written by the same man. Others conclude that John used an amanuensis or secretary when he wrote the Gospel.[1] Still others argue that the Gospel was written many years after the Revelation when its Aramaic-speaking author had gained a better mastery of Greek. All such solutions are hypotheses; we simply do not know with certainty what the answer is. We can only survey the facts and make educated judgments. *The solution of such problems does not affect the authority of inspired Scripture,* unless the author makes explicit affirmation in the book as to his identity. Otherwise these problems belong solely to the area of literary criticism.

Literary criticism is the study of such questions as the authorship, date, place of writing, recipients, style, sources, integrity, and purpose of any piece of literature. If the Bible had fallen directly from heaven, or had been verbally dictated by the Holy Spirit, literary criticism of the Bible would be irrelevant. If, however, the Holy Spirit used men in given historical situa-

1 See Rom. 16:22 for the practice of writing through a secretary; also Paul's personal salutations in I Cor. 16:21; Gal. 6:11; Col. 4:18; II Thess. 3:17, where he himself took up the pen to conclude his letters in his own hand.

tions to be vehicles of the Word of God, then we must try to recover that historical situation by asking critical questions. This is especially true if the Word of God for the entire church was given through the medium of a particular church facing specific problems. We cannot adequately understand the abiding message of God's Word until we have interpreted its particular immediate message in terms of the historical situation. When we study the letters of Paul addressed to individual churches, we must try to interpret what Paul wrote in terms of all we can recover about the situation in the church to which the letter is written.

To illustrate: It is far more profitable to study the epistles of Paul according to their place in Paul's travels, using them both to understand Paul's message to the several churches and to reconstruct Paul's relationships to the churches than to study them in their canonical order, which has neither historical nor theological significance.

This raises many interesting — and difficult — questions. For instance, we possess only two letters to the Corinthian church; but it is quite clear that Paul wrote four letters to Corinth. Letter A, referred to in I Corinthians 5:9, has not been preserved. Letter B is our I Corinthians. A third letter, which we may call letter C, is referred to in II Corinthians 2:3f.; 7:8, 12, which was painful for Paul to write and for the Corinthians to receive. Finally Paul wrote Letter D, our II Corinthians.

Has the painful letter (C), like A, been lost? Probably so. However, in II Corinthians 1:1-2:12, Paul explains why he is writing this fourth letter, and resumes this explanation in 7:5. The intervening section, 2:13-7:4, is an exalted passage which interrupts this historical narrative. Furthermore, the passage 6:14-7:1 is a small unit which has no coherence with its immediate context. This very uneven texture of II Corinthians, together with the references to letters not preserved, has led many scholars to the conclusion that II Corinthians, as it stands, does not represent the form in which Paul originally wrote it, but may include fragments from some of his lost correspondence. Questions like this, involving the "integrity" of a given work, that is, whether its present form is identical to its original form, are a legitimate and necessary exercise of literary criticism.[2]

The question of style cannot be overlooked. We have already met this problem in the Revelation of John and in the Fourth Gospel. The question of style is one of the most important considerations in the study of the Pastoral Epistles (I and II Tim. and Titus). We have enough letters that are unquestionably Paul's to be quite familiar with his literary style. When we analyze the language and idiom of the Pastorals, we find a rather different style. Not only are many of the key Pauline words absent, but numerous words not found in the other epistles appear. Perhaps the most telling stylistic fact in the Pastorals is the author's use of small connective words which are relatively unimportant in the message of the letters, but which are of particular importance because they are primarily stylistic in character. Because such words are not found in the other Pauline letters, many critics claim that this is strong evidence for the non-Pauline authorship of the Pastorals. Such questions must be faced, and convincing solutions can be supported only on the basis of the most exacting and thorough study. It cannot be overlooked, however, that these three letters claim to have been written by Paul, and the kind of stylistic distinctiveness in the Pastorals could be explained if Paul had used an amanuensis or secretary to whom he gave considerable freedom in the verbal formulation of these letters. If this is the case, the thought and some of the words in the Pastorals are Paul's but the rest of the words and the distinctive style are not Paul's, but his secretary's.

The most difficult area of literary criticism in the New Testament is that of the four Gospels, where we find two different

[2] For instance, the most casual reading of the apocryphal book of Enoch makes it self-evident that this book is a compilation of at least five separate works, with very different subject matter and theologies.

problems: that of the first three or Synoptic Gospels (so-called because they view the ministry of Jesus from the same perspective), and that of the Gospel of John which stands apart by itself. A completely uncritical view of the Gospels may regard them as four independent biographies of Jesus which intend to relate four supplementary accounts of the words and deeds of Jesus. From this perspective, the Gospels are viewed as chronicles of Jesus' travels and verbatim records of His preaching and teaching. That the first three Gospels have basically the same outline of Jesus' ministry and sequence of events is seen as proof that this is the way it happened. The three Gospels provide us, therefore, with three independent witnesses to the course of Jesus' ministry.

Where the reports of Jesus' words agree verbally, as they often do, the conclusion would seem obvious that they agree because we have verbatim accounts of Jesus' actual teaching. Where divergences appear, the simple uncritical solution is that Jesus said similar things on different occasions in somewhat different words. The historicity of Jesus and the integrity of His teaching is thus made to depend upon three independent accounts, which are taken to be practically equivalent to verbatim stenographic reports made on the scene by eyewitnesses.

From this popular point of view, the identity of the several Evangelists is of highest importance, for the Gospels must be the work of eyewitnesses whose testimony has the same kind of validity as an eyewitness in a modern court of law. It is true that a weighty tradition ascribes the First Gospel to the apostle Matthew, and the Second Gospel to John Mark, an attendant of the apostles (Acts 12:12, 25; 15:37, 39; II Tim. 4:11) and associate of Peter (I Pet. 5:13).

But the authority of the Gospels does not in fact rest upon either the report of immediate eyewitnesses or upon direct apostolic authorship, as the Third Gospel proves; for Luke was neither an eyewitness nor an apostle, but an author who carefully gathered material from apostolic eyewitnesses. Furthermore, none of the four Evangelists identifies himself. The specific authorship of the Gospels obviously was not an important matter at the time they were composed; and the identification of a given author with one of the Gospels is no part of the inspired text but must be settled on the basis of inferences drawn from both the external evidence of early Christian tradition and from the internal evidence drawn from the Gospels themselves.

The independence and direct apostolic authorship of the Gospels is probably the view of most laymen whose primary concern with the Bible is devotional; and the idea is widely held that unless the Gospels are three independent eyewitness accounts and practically stenographic reports of Jesus' mission and message, their witness to Jesus is seriously undermined. Furthermore, these first-century writings are often viewed from the perspective of modern copyright laws according to which one author's use of the work of another is plagiarism, which is of course ethically and legally abhorrent.

Four things must be said in reaction to this natural conclusion. First of all, in historical study, whether of the Bible or of Plutarch, Polybius, or Livy, a literature must be evaluated by the standards of its own age and culture and literary tradition, not by those of the present age. Ancient writers, including the biblical authors, must be studied in the light of ancient literary practices, not modern standards of copyright laws. One very common ancient literary practice was the free use of existing works. For example, the author of II Maccabees calmly informs his readers that his work is the condensation into a single readable volume of the massive five-volume work of Jason of Cyrene. He belabors the point of how much sweat and loss of sleep are demanded by this toil of abbreviating, and makes it his aim, as "the one who recasts the narrative," to strive for brevity of expression thus foregoing the exhaustive treatment of details demanded of the original historian (II Macc. 2:19-32). The author of II Maccabees happens to indicate his source; often writers used sources without any acknowledgment of that fact.[3]

It might be replied that a different standard of "literary honesty" is required of the Word of God, the Scripture inspired by the Spirit of truth. But this once again reflects the modern fear of plagiarism, and does not accept the obvious historical milieu in which the Word of God was given to men. The important question for those who hold the inspiration of the Bible is not, "What literary sources do its authors use?" but, "Do the authors use their sources so as to produce a true record?"

My colleague, Professor Everett F. Harrison, discusses this problem, pointing out that "nearly one-fifth of the Old Testament consists of deuterographs or repetitions of identical or very similar material. The most prominent example is the relations of Kings and Chronicles. . . . Therefore, if we are compelled on the basis of literary evidence to accept a theory of literary dependence, it should not be felt that this impugns the doctrine of inspiration. Originality is not a necessary qualification for Scripture."[4]

In the light of this ancient literary practice, it was not at all improper for one author to use sources without giving credit in documented footnotes or parenthetical references. As a matter of fact, we find in our Gospels a precise indication that such literary sources existed. Luke, apparently referring to the sources of information for his two-volume work (Luke-Acts), refers to "many" narratives already compiled, as well as to the witness of oral tradition coming from "eyewitnesses and ministers of the word" (Luke 1:1-2). Some scholars have felt that in these words, Luke expresses dissatisfaction with the records available to him and writes to produce a better narrative. This need not imply

[3] See G. A. Williamson's discussion of Josephus' use of sources, both acknowledged and unacknowledged, in his *The World of Josephus* (London: Secker & Warburg, 1964), chap. 19.

[4] E. F. Harrison, *Introduction to the New Testament* (Grand Rapids: Eerdmans, 1964), p. 145.

that these prior narratives were in error, only that they did not emphasize some things that Luke felt were important. He then felt free to use these written sources and supplement them from his own investigation of the Gospel tradition.

A second reaction to the theory of the interdependence of the Gospels is a theological one. If the Holy Spirit inspired one Gospel, it is not unnatural to conclude that the authors of other inspired Gospels might be led to make free use of prior inspired records. If, for instance, John Mark wrote down the substance of Peter's preaching, as tradition says, and did so under the guidance of the Holy Spirit so that he produced a trustworthy record of the meaning of Jesus' person and mission, we might expect that the Holy Spirit would lead Matthew and Luke to make use of this prior inspired apostolic record and base their own Gospels on it, even if (as is not clear) the apostle Matthew wrote the First Gospel and could also have drawn on his own independent recollections.

A third reaction is logical. If the Synoptic Gospels are in fact interdependent, that is, if one or two of the Evangelists made use of one or two of the others, does this not strengthen rather than weaken the trustworthiness of the Gospel tradition? If Matthew and Luke embodied the bulk of Mark's Gospel, and if Luke (and presumably also the first Evangelist, whether the apostle or someone else) in addition investigated the sources of oral tradition, as he suggests, this means nothing less than that Matthew and Luke place their imprimatur on the Gospel of Mark and on the common tradition they used. This point will carry even more weight if an apostle was actually the author of the First Gospel. By embodying Mark's Gospel in his own, he says in effect that Mark has written a trustworthy record of which he, Matthew, approves.

A fourth point is literary and historical, but also involves theology. One of the greatest problems in Synoptic study is that of divergences, sometimes minor, sometimes very significant, in the reported words of Jesus. One of the most striking illustrations is the account of the "Lord's Prayer."

Matthew 6:9-13	Luke 11:2-4
Our Father who art in heaven	Father
Hallowed be thy name	Hallowed be thy name
Thy kingdom come	Thy kingdom come
Thy will be done,	
on earth as it is in heaven	
Give us *this day*	Give us *each day*
our daily bread	our daily bread
And forgive us our *debts*	And forgive us our *sins*
as we also have forgiven our	*for we ourselves forgive*
debtors	*every one who is indebted*
	to us
And lead us not into temptation	And lead us not into temptation.
But deliver us from evil.[5]	

Here we have two different reports. Matthew has 57 words, Luke has 38. In the Greek, only 25 words agree precisely, 13 words are different. There can be no doubt that this is basically the same prayer; but it is found in very different settings in the two Gospels. Matthew includes it in the Sermon on the Mount; Luke places it toward the end of Jesus' ministry in a large block of material (Luke 9:51-18:14) inserted into the narrative structure between chapters nine and ten in Mark and between chapters eighteen and nineteen in Matthew.

It would be easy to assume that Jesus taught the same prayer on numerous occasions, two of which are recorded by Matthew and Luke. However, a closer study of the structure of the Gospels (which is discussed in the next chapter) makes it clear that their primary purpose is not to arrange the deeds and words of Jesus in their specific chronological order and setting. Furthermore, we must ask why Jesus would teach this basic prayer in several different forms, some longer, some shorter.

The nature of this problem becomes more precise when we recognize that in many other places, the words of Jesus are reported in obviously parallel passages but in quite different wording. It will be informative to list a few such parallel sayings

---

[5] The italicized words are different words in the two Gospels. The last verse in the AV of Matt. 6:13 is not a part of the oldest text but is a later addition.

to note the divergences. These are only a few illustrations, chosen at random; they can be multiplied at great length.

Matthew 5:4	*Luke 6:20*
1. Blessed are the poor in spirit, for theirs is the kingdom of heaven.	Blessed are you poor, for yours is the kingdom of God.

Matthew 5:6	*Luke 6:21*
2. Blessed are those who hunger and thirst for righteousness, for they shall be satisfied.	Blessed are you that hunger now, for you shall be satisfied.

Matthew 5:11	*Luke 6:22*
3. Blessed are you when men revile you and persecute you and utter all kinds of evil against you falsely on my account.	Blessed are you when men hate you, and when they exclude you and revile you, and cast out your name as evil, on account of the Son of Man.

Mark 3:29	*Matthew 12:32*
4. Whoever blasphemes against the Holy Spirit never has forgiveness, but is guilty of an eternal sin.	But whoever speaks against the Holy Spirit will not be forgiven, either in this age or in the age to come.

Mark 4:11	*Matthew 13:11*
5. To you has been given the secret of the Kingdom of God.	To you it has been given to know the secrets of the kingdom of heaven.

Mark 6:8	*Matthew 10:9*
6. He charged them to take nothing for their journey except a staff.	Take no gold, nor silver, nor copper in your belts, no bag . . . nor a staff.

Matthew 10:32	*Luke 12:8*
7. So everyone who acknowledges me before men, I will also acknowledge before my Father who is in heaven.	Everyone who acknowledges me before men, the Son of man will also acknowledge before the angels of God.

Matthew 11:12	*Luke 16:16*
8. From the days of John the Baptist until now, the kingdom of heaven has been coming violently (RSV^{mg}), and men of violence take it by force.	The law and the prophets were until John; since then the good news of the kingdom of God is preached, and everyone enters it violently.

Matthew 12:28	*Luke 11:20*
9. But if it is by the Spirit of God that I cast out demons, then the kingdom of God has come upon you.	But if it is by the finger of God that I cast out demons, then the kingdom of God has come upon you.

Matthew 13:19	*Mark 4:14*	*Luke 8:11*
10. When anyone hears the word of the kingdom.	The sower sows the word.	The seed is the word of God.

1 Cor. 11:25	*Matthew 26:28*	*Mark 14:24*	*Luke 22:20*
11. This cup is the new covenant in my blood.	This is my blood of the covenant, which is poured out for many for the forgiveness of sins.	This is my blood of the covenant, which is poured out for many.	This cup which is poured out for you is the new covenant in my blood.

These are only a few illustrations of the divergences which illustrate the nature of the "Synoptic problem." If the Gospels are completely independent records, meaning to provide the readers with precise accounts of the literal words of Jesus — His so-called *ipsissima verba* — the interpreter is faced with insuperable problems, for the wording of the three Gospels simply is not the same and cannot be forced into any harmonizing pattern of agreement. The simple fact is, a survey of such data as those listed above makes it quite clear that the Gospels *do not intend to provide us with a record of the precise literal words of Jesus.* On the contrary, the Evangelists feel free to expand, to interpret, to paraphrase, to bring out the meaning they see in Jesus' words; and they do this by varying His reported words, not by a technical apparatus of footnotes.

This procedure is quite intelligible if there is literary interdependence between the Gospels and these changes are made deliberately under the guidance of the Holy Spirit. Most of the variations above are inconsequential and do not affect the meaning of the words. In Nos. 1 and 2, Matthew brings out more clearly the deeper meaning of the simpler saying in Luke. In Nos. 3 and 7, the Son of Man is a title frequently used by our Lord and can therefore correctly be substituted for the personal pronoun. In No. 4, the meaning is the same, but Matthew uses the common Jewish idiom of the two ages, which Jesus Himself may well have used elsewhere. In No. 5, Jesus probably spoke of the central secret or newly revealed truth about the Kingdom; Matthew is interested in the variety involved in this new revelation — the several facets of meaning. No. 6 has two different wordings but basically the same meaning: that the disciples should go with an absolute minimum of equipment. Matthew's version of No. 8 is a difficult saying which Luke has simplified and clarified. In No. 9, Matthew makes more explicit the meaning of God's "finger" at work in the world; His "finger" is indeed the Holy Spirit.

No. 10 reflects an interesting variety. Mark probably preserves the most primitive form, for Luke's Gospel alone contains the idiom "the word of God" (Luke 5:1; 8:21; 11:28), and only Matthew uses the expression, "the word of the kingdom." Thus the Evangelists bear witness to the fact that the word of

Jesus is the word of the Kingdom, indeed, the very Word of God.

No. 11 is perhaps the most interesting, for we would expect that the words of institution of the Lord's Supper would be remembered and preserved with absolute precision. But not so. Matthew adds a phrase about forgiveness which is omitted by the other three accounts. Paul and Luke refer to the cup rather than the blood; Paul alone speaks of the "new covenant." This expression crept into the later Gospel tradition but is lacking in the best texts. These variations do not, however, affect the substance of the words of institution.

Variations like these provide an insoluble problem only for those who hold a dictation view of inspiration; but they are obvious facts which must be taken into consideration in understanding the nature of the Gospels and in the formulation of any doctrine of inspiration. They are facts which the Holy Spirit has implanted in the Word. To label such variations "errors" is to view the Gospels from a false perspective and to misunderstand what the Evangelists obviously intended to do, namely, to report accurately the substance of Jesus' teaching in meaningful terms to their readers, not to record His precise words in every instance. Thus Matthew, writing for Jewish Christians, alone preserves the Jewish idiom, "the kingdom of the heavens," while Mark and Luke convert it into the more meaningful idiom for Gentiles, "the kingdom of God."

We must now look more carefully at the first three Gospels to try to understand their literary interrelationship. The so-called Synoptic problem consists of a set of facts for which literary criticism tries to find a solution. First of all, about 90% of the material in Mark appears in Matthew. There are, in fact, only seven short passages in Mark which do not appear in Matthew; and there are only thirty verses in Mark which do not appear in Matthew and Luke. Furthermore, this similarity involves not only the general contents but also the very wording used, not only in the reports of the words of Jesus where similarity would be expected, but also in the narrative passages themselves. This is very important. The same kind of identity and diversity which appears in the recorded words of Jesus also occurs in the words which the Evangelists use to report Jesus' deeds.

This identity in wording is too close to be accidental. When three people write independent reports of the same event, the substance should be the same, but the wording will differ greatly as each man tells the story in his own words. If a teacher received two term papers in which the wording was identical page after page, he would be sure the students had worked together.

The force of the interdependence of the three Gospels can be demonstrated by the table on the following page. It is most unlikely that there would be so much exact identity of wording if the three Gospels were written independently.

For many years the prevailing view was that Matthew was the earliest Gospel and Mark abbreviated it. However, only a minority of critics support this theory today. It is an important fact that, although Mark is a shorter Gospel than Matthew, in many single units Mark is longer than Matthew, preserving details which Matthew omits. Furthermore, Mark's Greek is much rougher than Matthew's. It is easy to conceive of a rough style being polished when material is copied; but it is difficult to imagine a smooth style being converted into much poorer Greek, as would be the case if Mark used Matthew.

The strongest evidence is found in the order of material in the three Gospels. We will point out in the next chapter that the Evangelists do not intend to place much of their material, either narrative or didactic, in precise chronological order, but often arrange it topically. The outline of the main events of Jesus' career does indeed appear to be structured chronologically; but within this main course of development, events and units of Jesus' teaching are often grouped without specific chronological indications. In their ordering of events, the Gospels do not agree. This does not mean that the Gospels are in error or contradict each other; a contradiction can be claimed only

Matt. 21:23-37a	*Mark 11:27-33*	*Luke 20:1-5*
And when he entered into the temple the chief priests and the elders of the people came up to him as he was teaching and said, "By what authority are you doing these things, and who gave you this authority?" Jesus answered and said to them, "I will also ask you one question and if you will tell me the answer, then I also will tell you by what authority I do these things. The baptism of John, whence was it? From heaven or from men?" And they argued with one another saying, "If we say, 'From heaven,' he will say to us, 'Why then did you not believe him?' But if we say, 'From men,' we are afraid of the multitude; for all hold that John was a prophet." So they answered Jesus and said, "We do not know." And he said to them, "Neither will I tell you by what authority I do these things."	And they came again to Jerusalem. And as he was walking in the temple the chief priests and the scribes and the elders came to him and they said to him, "By what authority are you doing these things, or who gave you this authority to do them?" Jesus said to them, "I will ask you one question; answer me, and I will tell you by what authority I do these things. The baptism of John, was it from heaven or from men? Answer me." And they argued with one another saying, "If we say, 'From heaven,' he will say, 'Why then did you not believe him?' But shall we say, 'From men'? — and they were afraid of the multitude, for all held that John was a real prophet. So they answered Jesus and said, "We do not know." And Jesus said to them, "Neither will I tell you by what authority I do these things."	One day as he was teaching the people in the temple, and preaching the gospel, the chief priests and the scribes with the elders came up and said to him, "Tell us by what authority are you doing these things, or who is it that gave you this authority?" He answered and said to them, "I will also ask you a question; now tell me, The baptism of John, was it from heaven or from men?" And they discussed it with one another saying, "If we say, 'From heaven,' he will say, 'Why did you not believe him?' But if we say, 'From men,' all the people will stone us; for they are convinced that John was a prophet." So they answered that they did not know whence it was. And Jesus said to them, "Neither will I tell you by what authority I do these things."

if different Gospels state explicitly that given events took place at different times.

We may here give two illustrations to show the freedom with which the Evangelists arrange their narratives. Mark begins his Gospel with a series of events which occur in and around Capernaum. Matthew, on the other hand, begins by relating the calling of four of Jesus' disciples (4:18-22 = Mark 1:16-20) along with a summary statement that Jesus traveled throughout the towns of Galilee preaching and healing (4:23-25). Then he introduces at once a sample of Jesus' teaching, the Sermon on the Mount (chaps. 5-7). Matthew does this because he is especially interested in Jesus' words. After this sermon, Matthew relates a number of events to illustrate Jesus' deeds, especially His miracles of healing, grouping them together with very loose connective statements that do not tie them to specific times or places. The first incident is the healing of a leper (Matt. 8:1-4) which is paralleled in Mark 1:40-45. A subsequent incident is the healing of Peter's mother-in-law (Matt. 8:14-17), which Mark places before the healing of the leper (Mark 1:29-34). Why does Matthew reverse Mark's order? Somewhat later Matthew records the story of Jairus' daughter and the woman with the flow of blood (Matt. 9:18-26); this account stands much later in Mark (Mark 5:21-43).

Another illustration, whose purpose is discernible, is the way Luke introduces Jesus' ministry with the story of the rejection in Nazareth (Luke 4:16-30). Mark places this incident much later in Jesus' Galilean ministry (Mark 6:1-6). Luke does not mean to say this was the opening event in Jesus' Galilean ministry; he deliberately rearranges this material to sound the note of rejection at the very outset of Jesus' ministry. This is a legitimate procedure, and it could only be called "unhistorical" if Luke had specifically stated that this was the first event which occurred in Galilee.

When we recognize that the Gospels are not meant to be ar-

6 Small variations have been made from the RSV to bring out more clearly the similarity of the text.

ranged with chronological exactness in detail, the comparative relationship of the events in the three records becomes important in the study of their interrelationship. The order of events is determined not by the order in which these events happened, but by the Evangelists' interests and purpose in writing (see p. 168).

Three amazing facts emerge from the comparison of these three Gospels. First, Matthew and Luke follow Mark's order for the most part; second, in numerous specific points, as illustrated above, Matthew and Luke, in pursuing their own particular aims, depart from Mark's order of events; and, third, *Matthew and Luke never depart from Mark in the same way.* That is to say, Matthew and Luke never agree in their order of events over against Mark. When they differ, they do so in different ways. If Matthew were the oldest Gospel and had been used by Mark and Luke, there would certainly be places where Luke followed Matthew but Mark did not; but this phenomenon is never found. This fact establishes the priority of Mark with relative certainty. The Second Gospel provides the basic outline for the other two. However, since Mark's order is not determined primarily by historical chronology, neither the First nor the Third Gospel follows Mark slavishly; both feel free to vary his order as well as his wording. But Mark clearly provides the key to the problem of Synoptic interrelationship.

A second basic fact in the solution to the Synoptic question is the frequent agreement of Matthew and Luke, especially in discourses, where Mark has no material. The significance of this is found in the fact that such agreement between Matthew and Luke often involves precise verbal identity. If the reader opens two Bibles to the report of John's preaching in Matthew 3:7-10 and Luke 3:7-9, or to such a passage in the Sermon on the Mount as Matthew 6:25-34 and Luke 12:22-31, or to the healing of the centurion's servant in Matthew 8:5-13 and Luke 7:1-10, he will find both a striking identity of wording, accompanied by numerous variations, particularly in the addition or omission of material. Thus Luke 7:3-5 is lacking in the parallel account in Matthew; Matthew 8:11-12 is not found in the parallel passage in Luke 7, but in Luke 13:29-30.

These agreements of Matthew and Luke have led scholars to speak of a second source, along with Mark, which was used by the First and Third Gospels, which has been lost. This second source is designated by the letter Q, which stands for the German *Quelle,* meaning "source." Q is used to designate a lost document or source used by Matthew and Luke, and may well be included in the "many" accounts to which Luke refers in his opening sentences. There is not, however, the same general unanimity among scholars about Q as there is about the priority of Mark. Some think it was an actual single written document; others think that the first and third Evangelists possessed somewhat different editions or copies of Q, since there are many places where their parallel material differs considerably. Still others think the symbol Q represents only a source of oral tradition used by both Matthew and Luke. By the nature of the case, criticism can do no more than offer plausible theories to explain best these large areas of agreement between Matthew and Luke.

We have no proof that there ever was such an alleged document as Q. The facts here are not the same as with Mark. We have the Gospel of Mark which we can compare with Matthew and Luke, but we do not have the alleged document Q. And if we suppose that Q was a real document similar to the form in which many critics have reconstructed it, it would admittedly be impossible to reconstruct Mark by subtracting Q from Matthew and Luke.[7] Thus we conclude that while the priority of Mark is highly probable — indeed, in the judgment of the present writer, an established fact — the existence of an alleged document Q is only a possibility.[8]

---

[7] See above, p. 14.

[8] The reader should note that we are only trying to illustrate the questions raised by literary criticism, not to deal comprehensively with any question. However, we must note in passing that many scholars, following B. H. Streeter, recognize a "four-document" hypothesis. This theory recognizes not only Mark and Q, but two other alleged early documents, one used by

We may further illustrate the problem of literary criticism by discussing the question of the authorship of the first three Gospels. We must emphasize again that none of the Gospels is signed by its author, as are the letters of Paul. They are in fact anonymous writings. In this connection, it is a fact of great interest that the Gospels represent a new literary form in the ancient world. Paul's letters conform to the usual ancient fashion of epistolary writing. The ancient form of letter writing differed from that used now. First, the author's name was given, then the recipient's name, then a greeting, followed by the body of the letter. Paul follows this form uniformly.

Furthermore, the book of Acts is somewhat analogous to historical writing, although Luke's purpose is not to give a comprehensive history but to trace the development of certain selected aspects of the early church. However, in composing his two-volume work, Luke-Acts, the author follows the ancient convention of composing an introduction, Luke 1:1-4, which serves for both the Gospel and the Acts. This is followed in the second volume by a brief secondary introduction, Acts 1:1, which connects it with the first volume: "In the first book, O Theophilus, I have dealt with all that Jesus began to do and teach."

While there are many such similarities in literary form between the New Testament writings and secular literature, a Gospel represents a unique literary creation. The Hellenistic world knew the biographical literary form; but the Gospels do not conform to this pattern. They do not relate the outward history of a hero, nor the inner development of his character. They reflect little concern about detailed chronological sequence and

Matthew alone, designated M, and one used by Luke alone, designated L. This theory assumes that those materials found alone in Matthew and in Luke were embodied in two written documents which provided sources, along with Mark and Q, for the first and third Evangelists (B. H. Streeter, *The Four Gospels* [New York: Macmillan, 1925]). For a careful analysis of this question by an evangelical critic see Donald Guthrie, *New Testament Introduction* (Chicago: Inter-Varsity, 1965), I, chapter 5. In the judgment of the present author, the symbols M and L may conveniently be used to designate the material found alone in Matthew and Luke; but whether they represent written documents or bodies of oral tradition is unclear.

do not often fit their narrative into the precise historical setting. In short, their primary interest is not antiquarian or "historical," that is, to relate the career of a past important personage for its own sake. The Gospels relate the past because of its importance for the present. They purpose to show that the Jesus who lived and died was indeed the heavenly Lord now worshipped by the church — only His disciples did not recognize it at the time. If there had been no resurrection, there would have been no Gospels. As we will show in the next chapter, the very proclamation of Jesus' life, death, and resurrection, embodied finally in our Gospels, was itself the living Word of God. It is perhaps for this reason that the Evangelists felt no need to identify themselves or to try to provide authority for their literary products by their personal signature, as Paul often does (I Cor. 16:21; Gal. 6:11; Col. 4:18). The gospel about Jesus' life, death and resurrection had attained the status of the Word of God before it assumed written form, and therefore the Gospels did not require the authentication of their authors.

Nevertheless, modern scholarship is concerned about the historical questions. Who wrote each of the Gospels? When and where were they written? What was the purpose of the authors? The answer to these questions, which involves the exercise of literary criticism, is very difficult and must be sought by deducing inferences from a very complex body of data.

These available data are both external and internal. The New Testament writings enable us to trace with some accuracy the history of the church, at least in its main outlines, down to the fall of Jerusalem in A.D. 70. The period following that is relatively unknown, illuminated by only a few rays of light. An extant collection of writings produced by the (inaccurately) so-called Apostolic Fathers, such leaders of the church in the second century as Clement of Rome, Ignatius of Antioch, and Polycarp of Smyrna, reflects a knowledge of the Gospels, but is not very helpful for answering questions about the Gospels.

Our main source of information is a five-volume work by Papias, a bishop in the city of Hierapolis in Phrygia (in the

heart of Asia Minor). Unfortunately, this work, entitled, "Interpretations of the Words of the Lord," has been lost, except
for thirteen brief excerpts quoted by later authors, particularly
Irenaeus (*ca.* 185) and the historian Eusebius (died *ca.* 339).
From Papias comes the tradition: "Matthew composed the oracles (Logia) in the Hebrew tongue and everyone interpreted
them as he was able" (Eusebius, *Ecclesiastical History,* III, 39.
17). Papias also provides the source for the tradition about
the Second Gospel: "Mark became Peter's interpreter and
wrote accurately all that he remembered, not, indeed in order,
of the things said or done by the Lord. For he had not heard the
Lord, nor had he followed him, but later on, as I said, followed
Peter, who used to give teaching as necessity demanded but
not making, as it were, an arrangement of the Lord's oracles
(Logia) so that Mark did nothing wrong in writing down single
points as he remembered them" (Eusebius, III, 39.15). The
same tradition about Mark and Matthew is found in the
writings of later fathers, but their comments add little to what
is stated by Papias.

How trustworthy are these traditions? Are they conclusions
deduced from the Gospels themselves, and therefore of no independent value; or do they represent authentic independent
traditions which are credible? In evaluating these words of
Papias, critics come to very different conclusions. The tendency
in modern criticism is to ignore such traditions and to rest all
theories about authorship strictly on evidence drawn from the
Gospels themselves. However, since these are traditions which
cannot be readily deduced from the Gospels themselves, it seems
to be a sounder criticism to accept them as authentic, unless they
conflict with the internal data of the Gospels.

There is little if anything in the Second Gospel which would
suggest of itself that it was written by John Mark, or that it had
any connection with the preaching and teaching of the Apostle
Peter. It is, however, credible and consistent with the Gospel
that it was written in Rome and embodies the preaching of
Peter. When we read the Gospel to understand its central motif,

that is, the reason it was written, we find the central themes to be the divine person of Jesus, His conflict with the leaders of the Jews, and the events leading to His death. Jesus' death is so central to this Gospel that some scholars have called Mark a passion narrative with a long introduction explaining His death. A recent scholar has pointed out that Paul's letter to the Romans, written *ca.* A.D. 56 or 57, includes a very important section which has often been viewed as a sort of parenthesis to his main argument but which may in fact be understood as the heart of the epistle.[9] In Romans 9-11 Paul discusses at length the place of the Jewish people in God's redemptive program, in answer to the question, Why was the church in Rome primarily Gentile in character? What has become of God's promises to Israel? What is the relation of the church to Israel? Paul's answer is that believing Gentiles constitute the true people of God, the new Israel. The Jews had stumbled and fallen through rejection of their Messiah, but their place had been taken by the church, which consists largely of Gentiles.

Mark deals with a similar question. If Jesus was Messiah and Son of God, how did it happen that the Jews rejected and crucified Him? If He came to Israel, God's people, how did it come to pass that He was put to death on a Roman cross? How could it be if Jesus was indeed the resurrected and exalted Lord, recognized and now worshipped by the church, that He was rejected by the Jews and executed as a criminal by the Roman governor?

Mark shows how this conflict arose with the Jewish leaders because they would not recognize His exalted claims to forgive sins, to be lord of the Sabbath, to give a new authoritative teaching over against the scribal interpretation of the law. Even though He was the Son of God, they did not recognize it, but rejected Him and brought pressure on the Roman governor to have Him put to death. Romans would understand why a weak governor, desiring only to keep the peace, would be willing to put to death an innocent man accused of sedition (Mark 15:15.

9 Stephen Neill, *The Interpretation of the New Testament 1861-1961* (London: Oxford, 1964), p. 184.

This verse appears only in Mark). It is reasonable to conclude that the tradition is right in saying that this Gospel was written in Rome.

Furthermore, the language of Mark is rougher Greek than that of the First or Third Gospels. It preserves several Aramaic expressions (Mark 7:34; 5:41), and has a number of Semitic grammatical idioms which are smoothed up by the other two Evangelists. This language suits the Papian tradition about the Markan authorship. There is, therefore, no strong reason to reject the tradition from Papias about Mark, since he was a companion of Peter (I Pet. 5:13), and we are quite sure from references in the Apostolic Fathers that Peter did visit Rome.

With the tradition about the First Gospel, the problem is more difficult. Papias tells us that Matthew wrote the Oracles (Logia) in Aramaic which were later translated into Greek. The first problem here is the meaning of the word "Logia." Many scholars have concluded that this word designated the teachings of Jesus, and that Matthew was the compiler of a collection of didactic materials, possibly Q, which was later embodied in the Gospel. However from Papias' use of the term elsewhere, it is more likely that by Logia, he means a Gospel, not merely a collection of teachings.

Could our Gospel have been written first in Aramaic and then translated into Greek? At first thought, it seems unlikely, for the Gospel is written in smooth idiomatic Greek, free from the Aramaic idioms which appear in Mark. However, this does not rule out the possibility of an Aramaic original, for Josephus, the contemporary Jewish historian, by his own admission did precisely this, writing his *Jewish War* first in Aramaic and later translating it into Greek. Yet the Greek version of Josephus is almost completely free from Aramaic idioms.

However, the question in the case of Matthew is even more complicated. As we have indicated, it is almost certain that the Gospel of Matthew as we have it has made use of the Gospel of Mark as its main source and has embodied a large percentage of the Second Gospel in his work. This raises two questions:

Could an author have first written an Aramaic Gospel and then neglected it in favor of another Gospel, Mark, when writing a Greek version? And would an apostle have made such extensive use of a Gospel not written by an apostle when he had his own memory and apostolic authority to draw on?

These two problems have in the judgment of most modern critics weighed strongly against the theory of Matthean authorship (and we must remember that it is a theory, not a fact of sacred Scripture). In meeting the first difficulty, elaborate hypotheses have been devised to account for two different editions of Matthew's Gospel — one in Aramaic, based on his own memory, and a second one in Greek which made use of Mark. Our judgment is that this seems highly unlikely; such a theory is too complicated to be persuasive. At this point, we must conclude that Papias was in error when he said that our Matthew was originally written in Aramaic.

Does this mean that he was also in error about the alleged Matthean authorship? To put the question in another way, could an apostle have made use of a non-apostolic Gospel, as Matthew appears to have used Mark? In answer to this, we can only suggest hypotheses; we do not have facts to establish a solution. One fact does seem clear: Matthew was written for a Jewish Christian community to show that Jesus was indeed the fulfilment of the promises to Israel, that He was the Jewish Messiah but in a different role from that expected by the Jews, that He had brought the Kingdom of God to men, that He had fulfilled the Old Testament law. A majority of scholars feel that the most likely place for such a Gospel to have been written was in Syria in a city such as Antioch where there was a mixed congregation of both Gentiles and Jews in the church.

Historical imagination can easily understand how, in such a situation, an apostle could have made extensive use of Mark's prior Gospel. A passage in Paul's letter to the Galatians (Gal. 2:11ff.) proves that there were tensions between Jewish and Gentile Christians in Antioch which involved the person and authority of Peter. It is very possible that the arrival of the

Gospel of Mark in Antioch a decade or more later, bearing the oral authority of Peter's witness to the person and mission of Jesus, was used by the Gentile wing of the church in their own interests against the Jewish wing. If so, an apostle, Matthew, could very well have produced a Gospel of his own in which he embodied practically the entire bulk of Peter's Gospel (thus demonstrating his essential agreement with Peter's witness) and at the same time added much new material, of which he himself may well have been the compiler. His purpose would be to show that while Peter's record was correct, it did not tell the whole story. Jesus was indeed the Messiah and Son of God; He was also the King of Israel; He fulfilled the Old Testament hope; He reinterpreted the meaning of the Jewish law, thereby fulfilling it; and He brought into being a circle of Jewish disciples who were destined to become the nucleus of His church, the true people of God, for whom the Old Testament, as fulfilled in Him, possessed abiding validity. Thus even though Israel rejected her Messiah and the Jewish state suffered God's judgment in the destruction of A. D. 70, there is an inescapable element of continuity between Israel and the church. Admittedly, all this is hypothesis, but it is hypothesis which tries to make historical sense of the facts, both external and internal, which are at our disposal.

The external tradition that Luke-Acts was written by Luke, a companion of Paul, does not do violence to the internal evidence of that two-volume work. The so-called "we-sections" of Acts (16:10-16; 20:5-21; 27:1-28:16), where the narrative changes from the third to the first person, suggest that the author was a companion of Paul on these three occasions and is drawing upon his own notes for his source material. The purpose of Luke-Acts is broader than that of either Mark or Matthew. It is to explain to one Theophilus (Luke 1:1, Acts 1:1), apparently a Gentile Christian, how a small Jewish messianic movement in a corner of the Roman Empire issued in a Gentile congregation in the Roman capital with its chief representative a prisoner of the emperor. The important question for Luke is: What is the rela-

tionship of this movement to the Gentile authorities? Thus
Luke places both the mission of Jesus and the emergence of the
church in a broader historical and political perspective. He is
interested in the relationship of the gospel to non-Jews, especially
to civic and political authorities. There is no good reason to reject the tradition about Luke.

Criticism has found a particularly difficult problem in ac-
counting for the Fourth Gospel, because it is very different from
the Synoptics. We shall here indicate only some of the outstanding differences. The first is in geography. The Synoptics
agree in placing the ministry of Jesus in Galilee, with a journey
to Jerusalem at the end which led to His death. John relates
very little of the Galilean ministry (see John 2:1-12; 4:43-54; 6:1-
7:1), but he narrates a series of events and discourses in Jerusalem
when Jesus was in the capital city at the time of the Jewish
feasts (2:13; 5:1; 7:2; 10:22; 11:55).

The style of Jesus' teaching recorded by John is different
from the short pithy sayings, vivid figures of speech, and parables which fill the Synoptics. John structures Jesus' teaching
in long, flowing discourses. The difference in the style of the
Greek is equally striking. This is difficult to perceive in English,
but everyone who reads Mark in Greek and then turns to John
is struck by the simplicity and ease of the latter, with its simple
sentences connected by "and" (paratactic style), and its limited
vocabulary. Furthermore, the style of the Fourth Gospel is
also the style of the Epistles of John.

The most important difference between John and the Synoptics is that of theological content. The proclamation of the
Kingdom of God in the Synoptics is displaced by eternal life
in John. He refers to the Kingdom of God only in chapter 3:3, 5.
Furthermore, when eternal life appears in the Synoptics, it is not
portrayed as a present possession but the life of the Age to
Come (Matt. 19:16, 23, 28, 29; 25:46), to be inherited at the
glorious appearing of the Son of Man in His Kingdom. In John,
life is a present possession brought to men here and now (John
3:36; 5:24; 10:10; 21:31). Can a Gospel so very different from

the Synoptics accurately reflect the mission and message of Jesus? Can it have had any connection with either an apostle or an eyewitness?

This Gospel, like the others, is anonymous (John 21:24) ; but external tradition attributes it to the Apostle John. Irenaeus, who became bishop of Lyons in Gaul in A.D. 177, tells that he often heard Polycarp, the bishop of Smyrna who was martyred in A.D. 155, relate what he had heard from the lips of John and the other disciples about Jesus. This is a very strong line of connected testimony; and Irenaeus tells us that John published the Gospel in Ephesus. Critical scholars recognize that if it were not for the great differences between John and the Synoptics, there would be no reason for questioning the credibility of such a strong witness. However, is it possible that an apostle who had himself been an eyewitness and auditor of Jesus could have written a Gospel so very different from the Synoptics? This is the crucial critical question.

The differences in locale are not insurmountable. It is quite possible that Jesus made a number of journeys to Jerusalem at the time of the feasts when He engaged in discussion with the rabbis and priests in the capital city. In fact, the words in Matthew 23:37, "O Jerusalem . . . *how often* would I have gathered your children together as a hen gathers her brood," suggest that Jesus had had far more contacts with Jerusalem than the Synoptics record.

The difference in style is more difficult. One could argue that Jesus used a different style in Jerusalem among the learned men of the Jews than He used in Galilee among the common people, but this theory does not completely solve the problem, for the discourse on the bread of life in John 6:25ff., which follows the miracle of the feeding of the 5000 in Galilee has a typically "Jerusalem" rather than Galilean style. The problem is heightened by the similarity in style between the discourses of Jesus in the Fourth Gospel and the language of John in the First Epistle, and by the fact that in John 3 it is impossible to be sure precisely where John stops relating the teaching of Jesus and begins with his own commentary.

One solution to this problem would seem to be that John is not attempting to relate the exact words of Jesus. Rather, he is recording the substance and the deeper meaning of Jesus' teachings as he, the inspired apostle, understood and interpreted them. We have already seen that a process of interpretation was at work in the Synoptic Gospels — a process which we may believe was inspired and superintended by the Holy Spirit Himself. If the Gospel was written, as tradition asserts, near the end of the century when John was an old man, we may well imagine John for years remembering, pondering, brooding over the teachings of Jesus, until a mutual interaction occurred. John's mind became saturated with the remembered teachings of Jesus so that the form of Jesus' teaching also became adapted in his own mind to John's own idiom, until at last, a single style resulted in which the form of Jesus' words and the idiom of John himself are merged. The result is a "spiritual" Gospel which brings out the true significance of Jesus' person and mission more profoundly than the Synoptics do. This is not to suggest that John invented the events he recorded. The comment in John 6:15, lacking in the Synoptics, that after the miracle of the feeding of the five thousand the people wanted to force Jesus to assume the role of messianic King, is one of the soundest and most meaningful historical references in all four Gospels.

The apparent difference in theological content must be admitted honestly. This does not mean that John contradicts the Synoptics, as has frequently been argued. The difference is one of emphasis, not of basic content. The central theme of the preaching of Jesus in the Synoptics is the coming of the Kingdom of God (Mark 1:15). The final meaning of this announcement is the glorious establishment of God's kingly rule on earth when all evil is destroyed, the dead raised, and God's people brought into perfect fellowship with Him. This consummation will be accomplished only by the glorious coming of the heavenly Son of Man — the event today spoken of as the second coming of Christ (Matt. 13:41-43; Mark 13:26-27; Matt. 25:31ff.). It is an eschatological event, which means the end of the world as we know it and the inauguration of the world to come. In the Synoptics, the life of this future age to be inaugurated by the coming of the Kingdom of God is called eternal life. The rich young ruler asked how he might inherit eternal life (Matt. 19:16). In answer, Jesus speaks about entering the Kingdom of Heaven (v. 23), about inheriting eternal life when the Son of Man shall come to sit on His glorious throne (vv. 28, 29); and the parallel passage in Mark speaks of the life of the Age to Come (Mark 10:30). Luke 20:35 makes it clear that this life of the future age is resurrection life when God's people enter into immortality.

Although the Synoptics nowhere speak of eternal life as something present, the most significant and central fact in Jesus' preaching is that the Kingdom of God, which belongs to the Age to Come, has already come to men (Matt. 12:28), is already among them (Luke 17:20), and must be received here and now (Mark 10:15). While the consummation of all that God's kingly rule means awaits the end of the age and the coming of the Son of Man in glory, Jesus, the Son of Man, has already appeared among men, bringing to them the blessings of the Kingdom of God: forgiveness (Mark 2:10-11), joy (Mark 2:18-19), salvation (Luke 19:9), righteousness (Matt. 6:33), deliverance from demonic bondage (Matt. 12:28), fellowship (Luke 15:1-2, 23, 24).

This is precisely the meaning of the Fourth Gospel's teaching about eternal life. In John, as in the Synoptics, this life is the life of the Age to Come. John 12:25 says, "He who hates his life in this world will keep it for eternal life." "This world" stands in contrast to the world to come; and eternal life is the life of the world to come. The "hating" of one's life means, as in the Synoptics, that one's love for the Kingdom of God must take priority over all other claims, even over one's own life (Luke 14:26). It is equivalent to forsaking everything, if necessary, life itself, for the sake of the Kingdom of God. The theology of John 12:25 is the same as that of Mark 10:29-31.

If the Synoptic Gospels teach that the Kingdom of God, which belongs to the world to come, has come to men in the midst of human history, bringing to them its blessings, John emphasizes one aspect of the presence of the Kingdom: its gift of life. For John, the greatest blessing of the Kingdom is eternal life; and this life, along with its other blessings, has come to men because the Kingdom of God itself has come. Thus although there is an admitted difference of emphasis, the theological content is the same. There is no contradiction. To be born again in order to enter the Kingdom of God (John 3:3, 5) is the same as receiving the Kingdom of God like a little child in order to enter the Kingdom (Mark 10:15), as turning and becoming like a little child (Matt. 18:3).

A critical survey of the differences between John and the Synoptics does not invalidate the tradition that the Gospel stems from the Apostle John. As W. F. Albright, one of the greatest living biblical scholars, has said,

> There is absolutely nothing to show that any of Jesus' teachings have been distorted or falsified, or that any vital new element has been added to them. . . . One of the strangest assumptions of critical New Testament scholars and theologians is that the mind of Jesus was so limited that any apparent contrast between John and the synoptics must be due to differences between early Christian theologians. Every great thinker and personality is going to be interpreted differently by different friends and hearers, who will select what seems most congenial or useful out of what they have seen and heard.[10]

There is no compelling reason to reject the soundness of Irenaeus' testimony about the authorship of the Fourth Gospel.

These are the kinds of questions with which literary criticism must occupy itself. The devotional reader must come to the

10 "Recent Discoveries in Palestine and the Gospel of John," in W. D. Davies and D. Daube, eds., *The Background of the New Testament and its Eschatology* (Cambridge: University Press, 1950), pp. 170f.

Bible and read it as God's Word speaking directly to him. However, since God has given us His Word through historical men and processes, both the scholar and the thoughtful layman must be concerned to ask such questions as those discussed in this chapter.

CHAPTER VI

Form Criticism

IN THE PRECEDING CHAPTER, WE HAVE DISCUSSED THE NATURE OF the Synoptic problem, and have indicated that the prevailing solution, namely, the two-source hypothesis, appears to be based upon enough factual evidence to be accepted as a literary fact. We have further attempted to show that this prevailing solution involving interdependence is in no way incompatible with a "high" view of inspiration. We have concluded further that the strength of the threefold witness of the Synoptic Gospels to the person and mission of Jesus is not weakened by such interdependence. It is a fallacious logic to argue that literary independence between the Evangelists leads to the formula, $1 + 1 + 1 = 3$ witnesses, while literary interdependence leads to the formula, $1 \times 1 \times 1 = 1$ witness. On the contrary, this very literary interdependence reflects the confidence of both Matthew and Luke in the soundness of Mark's record and of the second source, Q. This means that we have a threefold evangelical attestation to the soundness of Mark's portrait of Jesus.

The solution to the Synoptic problem was not achieved by scholars who held a high view of the Bible but by men who were concerned primarily with historical and literary questions. These men felt that only because they had been set free from any dogmatic view of biblical inspiration were they able to deal freely with the Gospels as historical documents. However, as we have pointed out in the second chapter, the scholars of this period were not as objective as they thought but interpreted the Bible from a liberal point of view. In the earliest documents, Mark and Q, these scholars felt they had at last discovered the true historical Jesus, who was a prophet of the highest ethico-spiritual ideals the race has known. The Christian gospel was thus thought to be secured by the findings of historical criticism. Elements such as the pre-existence and deity of Christ, His incarnation, His virgin birth, which were distasteful to the liberal critic, but which are emphasized in John and in the early chapters of Matthew and Luke, were thrust aside as irrelevant for the gospel. Undoubtedly here is one of the reasons why evangelicals have held a strongly negative attitude toward biblical criticism as such. Since the critical method was coupled with a liberal theology, the mistaken conviction arose that criticism itself is a liberal discipline.

The confidence of the "old liberals" that in these oldest literary sources, Mark and Q, they had discovered a purely "historical," i.e., non-supernatural, Jesus was soon shattered from two different directions. On the one side Albert Schweitzer made it quite clear that the historical Jesus was no mere ethical prophet teaching men to love God and one another. At the heart of Jesus' message was the announcement that human history would end in a mighty cosmic catastrophe when He would be elevated to the supernatural role of a heavenly Son of Man who would come to earth from heaven with clouds of glory to preside over the judgment of the race. Such apocalyptic ideas did not fit the liberal understanding of God, man, and history, but reflected the hopes of ancient Jewish apocalyptists. The "historical Jesus," as Schweitzer reconstructed Him, could not provide a historical basis for Christian faith, as the liberals thought; for what Jesus taught was impossible for modern man to believe.

On the contrary, "the historical knowledge of the personality and life of Jesus will not be a help, but perhaps even an offence to religion. . . . Jesus as a concrete historical personality remains a stranger to our time,"[1] because He was a deluded fanatic who died in blind devotion to a mad apocalyptic dream which was never realized and which, for a modern man like Schweitzer, never can be realized.

About the same time an attack came from another direction. William Wrede found in the Gospels, particularly in Mark, not the liberal ethical prophet of love and brotherhood, but a divine Messiah who was fully self-conscious of being the Son of God. Wrede shared the same view of the nature of history as the liberals; the historical Jesus must have been a man capable of being understood exclusively in "historical," that is, human non-supernatural categories. Historical criticism has no categories to deal with such alleged phenomena as incarnate deity and divine men. However, Wrede departed from the liberals in his understanding of the portrait of Jesus in Mark. The liberals held that the Jesus of Mark was quite "historical"; Wrede insisted that the Jesus of Mark was "unhistorical" and supernatural. However, this supernatural Jesus cannot be identical to the Jesus who lived in history. Mark is, therefore, not historically reliable and does not picture accurately the historical Jesus. Wrede concluded that the divine Christ pictured in Mark reflects the faith of the church a generation after Jesus lived; that the historical, non-messianic, non-divine Jesus has been hidden behind the divine portrait of Mark. Wrede not only analyzed the portrait of the divine Christ in Mark; he went further to attempt to explain how the human Jesus in history became the divine Christ in Mark. This he does by his famous theory of the Messianic Secret.[2] Although this theory has not been widely accepted, Wrede's conclusion that Mark portrays

---

[1] Albert Schweitzer, *The Quest of the Historical Jesus* (London: Black, 1911) , p. 399.

[2] Wrede's book, published in 1913, has not been translated into English. It is entitled *Das Messiasgeheimnis in den Evangelien* ("The Messianic Secret in the Gospels") . See pp. 157f. for an examination of this theory.

a divine Messiah is generally acknowledged as sound. Since a divine Messiah is not palatable to the modern scientific historical perspective, criticism asked where a human historical Jesus could be found. How did the human Jesus of history become the divine Christ of Mark?

This problem contributed to the emergence of a new method of Gospel study called form criticism *(Formgeschichte)*. Since our earliest Gospel sources were written probably not earlier than A.D. 60, a generation elapsed when the traditions about Jesus, the stories of His deeds, and the reports of His words were preserved by the church in oral form. Back of the earliest written Gospel stands a generation of the proclamation of the gospel in oral form. Form criticism must be based upon our written Gospels, for we have no other sources or reliable traditions about Jesus. But form critics analyzed the Gospels in order to recover the process by which the original, purely historical tradition was transformed into the supernaturally colored tradition as it is embodied in the written Gospels which we have today. To express this in the words of a contemporary form critic, "The work of the Form Critics was designed to show that the message of Jesus as given to us by the synoptists is, for the most part, not authentic but was minted by the faith of the primitive Christian community in its various stages."[3]

The designation "form criticism" refers to the various literary forms which the oral tradition assumed as it was passed from mouth to mouth. Back of this study was the assumption that certain laws of oral tradition when applied to the Gospels will lead to the recovery of the earliest form of the tradition. A close study of these forms led to the critical conclusion that in its earliest stages, the material in the Gospels was passed on orally as a series of disconnected units, anecdotes, stories, sayings, teachings, parables, and so on. Each unit of tradition had its own history in the church. The historical outline of Jesus'

[3] Ernst Käsemann, *Essays on New Testament Themes* (Naperville, Ill.: Allenson, 1964), p. 15. We must recognize that many scholars practice form criticism without assuming such radical presuppositions.

career as it is found in Mark and largely embodied in Matthew and Luke is no part of this tradition, but is the creation of the author of the Second Gospel, who collected many of these units of tradition, created a historical outline for Jesus' career, and used this outline as a narrative thread upon which to string the disconnected beads of independent traditions. This means that the indications in the Gospels of sequence, time, place, and the like are quite unhistorical and untrustworthy and must therefore be ignored by serious Gospel criticism. As a result, we have no "life" or "biography" of Jesus, but only a series of detached anecdotes and teachings artificially and unhistorically strung together.

Furthermore, as these units, or pericopes, were passed on in the church by word of mouth, both their literary form and their content were modified in accordance with the laws of oral tradition and were made to conform to the needs and life of the Christian community. Each pericope as it stands in written form represents the end of a process of transformation from the historical Jesus to the believing Christian church of A.D. 60-90. The Gospels in their present form are not the records of a historical Jesus, nor the products of contemporary reporters who wrote down what they saw Jesus do and heard Him say. They are the product of the believing Christian church of a generation later, and they reflect the life and faith of that community rather than the actual situation of Jesus' life. The life setting (*Sitz im Leben*) of the Gospel traditions as we have them is the Christian church of A.D. 60-90. The Gospels are not neutral, impartial, objective reports of disinterested, uncommitted observers, but are the product of Christian believers and reflect their faith. To them, Jesus was the Messiah, the divine Son of God, the heavenly Son of Man; and this faith is so reflected in the Gospels that it has in fact transformed the historical Jesus into the divine Christ of faith.

Thus the form critics found in the Gospels a testimony to the life and faith of the Christian community which produced them rather than to the deeds, words, and person of the historical Jesus. This does not mean that there is nothing of historical worth in the Gospels, for at the beginning of the process is admittedly a sound historical tradition. This historical base was however so transformed in a generation of oral repetition that only through the exercise of form criticism can one sift out the trustworthy historical residue from the later unhistorical accretions.

We must emphasize again that not all form critics find a complete transformation of the Gospel tradition. Vincent Taylor, for instance, has written one of the best books in English on form criticism, but he holds a rather high view of the trustworthiness of the historical tradition. The opposite extreme is illustrated by Rudolf Bultmann who has concluded that the nature of our Gospels is such that we can now know almost nothing about the life and personality of Jesus.[4]

We shall illustrate how form criticism deals with a few units in the Gospels. The pericope about the founding of the church, (Matt. 16:17-19) cannot be historical, for the "historical Jesus" did not think of Himself as one with a divine mission to bring into existence a new people — the church. He was an apocalyptic Jewish prophet whose mission and message were concerned only with the Jewish people. Matthew 16:17-19 represents an attempt by the church to vindicate its existence by an unhistorical attributing of its ultimate origin to Jesus. The *Sitz im Leben* of this passage is not the life and teachings of the historical Jesus but the Christian church which believed itself to be the *Ekklesia,* the new people of God, founded by Jesus.

A verse such as Mark 13:10 = Matthew 24:14 which places on the lips of Jesus a prophecy of the world-wide Christian mission cannot be historically reliable, for Jesus could not foresee the future, did not believe that the world would last long, and had no purpose to found a church. This again is only a saying created by Christian tradition to vindicate its own mission in the Gentile world by attributing it to Jesus.

4 See Vincent Taylor, *The Formation of the Gospel* (London: Macmillan, 1935) ; R. Bultmann, *Jesus and the Word* (New York: Scribner's, 1926) , p. 8.

The parable of the five wise and five foolish maidens in Matthew 25:1-13 cannot be authentic as it stands, for it is an allegory about the church which predicts in parabolic form the judgment which will separate true and false Christians at the end of the world. Originally, Jesus must have told some such parable to warn the Jews of impending disaster if they did not respond to His message; but the church transformed an original parable into an allegory to explain the delay of the expected immediate end of the world and the coming of the Son of Man (see especially verse 5, "as the bridegroom was delayed").

These are only a few isolated illustrations. At the hands of extreme form critics, the Gospels lose much of their trustworthiness as historical records, and the picture of Jesus is lost. The Son of God incarnate in Jesus of Nazareth becomes a product rather than the creator of Christian faith. He is no longer seen as the Saviour of the Christian community. One of the "post-Bultmannians" clearly expresses this radical skepticism of the form critics: "It was not historical but kerygmatic interest which handed them [the individual units of Gospel tradition] on. From this standpoint it becomes comprehensible that this tradition, or at least the overwhelming mass of it, cannot be called authentic. Only a few words of the Sermon on the Mount and of the conflict with the Pharisees, a number of parables and some scattered material of various kinds go back with any degree of probability to the Jesus of history himself. Of his deeds, we know only that he had the reputation of being a miracle-worker, that he himself referred to his power of exorcism and that he was finally crucified under Pontius Pilate."[5]

Little wonder that evangelicals with a high view of the Bible and of Christ have felt that form criticism could be nothing but an enemy of the Christian faith as evangelicals understand it. But the skepticism expressed by Käsemann is shared by only a relatively small, albeit influential, group of "radical" critics; and this skepticism is not a result of the method by itself but of form criticism coupled with a rationalistic view of the nature

[5] Ernst Käsemann, *op. cit.,* pp. 59f.

of history. We meet here a situation analogous to that of the literary criticism of the Synoptic Gospels. Because the solution of the Synoptic problem was coupled with a liberal theology with its portrait of the ethical prophet of love, conservatives often felt that literary criticism must itself be an instrument of a liberal theology. Now, however, most evangelical New Testament scholars have recognized the validity of the "documentary hypothesis," viz., that Matthew and Luke made use of Mark and Q; and we have shown in the preceding chapter that this critical solution is in no way hostile to an evangelical faith.

The same thing is true of form criticism. Despite the radical use which has been made of this method, it contains valid elements. To discover them, we must look again at the Gospels and try to discover precisely what they claim for themselves. Our final authority is the Gospels themselves, not theories about them; and we must try to sort out the apparent historical literary facts from the unwarranted, unproven assumptions held by the extreme form critics. When this is done, we will find that at the most crucial point form criticism, in spite of many form critics, in fact supports an evangelical faith.

First, it is quite certain that the gospel was in fact preserved for a generation in oral form before it was reduced to writing. A New Testament scholar standing in the liberal tradition recently published a book which defends the view that Jesus called Matthew, the tax collector, because of his skill with the pen, and Matthew wrote down many of Jesus' words as he heard them delivered.[6] This we would like to believe; but such a theory, as attractive to an evangelical faith as it is, simply does not square with the data of the Gospels.

When we examine Luke's prologue, we find Luke distinguishing between (1) his own Gospel, (2) other written records (which we may assume Luke used), and (3) those things "delivered to us by those who from the beginning were eyewitnesses and ministers of the word" (Luke 1:1-2). First was the oral

6 Edgar J. Goodspeed, *Matthew, Apostle and Evangelist* (Philadelphia: Winston, 1959).

tradition which was handed down by eyewitnesses and ministers of the word, probably the apostles; then came the written records, based on this oral tradition; then came Luke's own Gospel.

The fact that we must reckon with a period of oral traditions before we have written Gospels is further supported by the use of several key words throughout the New Testament. Let us examine the word "gospel" (Greek, εὐαγγέλιον). This word is not used to designate written records, that is, our four Gospels, in the New Testament, but is found considerably later in the second century. Before "gospel" was used of written records it was used of oral proclamation.

Εὐαγγέλιον means "good news." The gospel is first of all the message which Jesus preached, which is called "the gospel of God." Men are called upon to believe this good news (Mark 1: 14-15). This gospel is the oral proclamation by Jesus that the time of salvation promised by the prophets is fulfilled, and "the Kingdom of God is at hand." This means that God is about to act in Jesus' mission to establish His divine rule among men. The designation of good news as the "gospel of God" does not mean that it is new truth about God, but good news that comes from God. God is going to do something in the mission of Jesus Christ for man's salvation. The gospel is also the "good news about the Kingdom of God" (Matt. 4:23; 9:35). When Mark introduces his story of Jesus with the words, "The beginning of the gospel of Jesus Christ" (Mark 1:1), "gospel" does not refer to the written record itself but to the message embodied in Mark's record, that is, the good news about the salvation God has accomplished in Jesus Christ.

"Gospel" occurs frequently in the epistles; and it always refers to the good news of the salvation wrought in Jesus Christ. Paul proclaimed this good news orally on his missionary travels, and then he expounded the gospel in written form in his letters to the several churches. Paul had preached the good news of salvation both in word and in power (I Thess. 1:5). There is only one true gospel, although there are other messages which claim to be the gospel (Gal. 1:6-9). The true gospel is not a human invention, nor does it have its origin with men, but with Jesus Christ (Gal. 1:11-12). At the same time, this good news of God's saving work in Christ is a tradition handed down by men. The Corinthians received the gospel from Paul (I Cor. 15:1), who had in turn received it from his spiritual predecessors (I Cor. 15:3). This gospel was the good news that Christ died for our sins, was buried and rose again on the third day.

Thus the proclaimed gospel is viewed as a *tradition* originating with God's redeeming purpose, given substance by the person and work of Jesus, and handed down by the apostles. Paul exhorts the Thessalonians to hold fast the traditions they had received from the apostles, whether these were transmitted orally or by written word (II Thess. 2:15). The noun rendered "traditions" (παράδοσις) has the companion verb "deliver" (παραδίδωμι) which is also used in I Corinthians 15:3, "For I *delivered* unto you . . . what I also received." The same idiom of a handed-down tradition is found in the words of Jude, who writes of "the faith which was once for all delivered (παραδίδοναι) to the saints" (Jude 3).

The idiom describing the transmission of the oral Gospel tradition is the same idiom used to describe the oral interpretations of the law made by the scribes, which are called "the traditions of the elders" (Matt. 15:2ff.). These oral traditions were developed over many years, were memorized and passed on from scribal teachers to disciples, and finally assumed written form in the Mishnah in the second century of our era.

Many form critics assume that the Gospel tradition like the scribal tradition must be regarded as a purely human phenomenon, following the same laws of transmission. However, there is a further, all-important factor which cannot be left out of consideration, and which, if true, places the Gospel tradition in a distinctive light. *The tradition of the scribes is regarded as a human tradition which frustrates the Word of God* (Matt. 15:6), whereas the Gospel tradition is itself the Word of God.

It can be answered that this belief of the Christian church only parallels the belief of the Pharisees that their oral traditions were also the Word of God and part of the Mosaic law. This was the distinctive element in the Pharisaic beliefs. The students of the law had developed the elaborate oral tradition in the effort to interpret and to apply the law in their day. They held the view that this oral law, as well as the written law, had been given to Moses and that both bodies of law, written and oral, had been preserved through the centuries. Concerning this oral law, we read, "Moses received the Law from Sinai and committed it to Joshua, and Joshua to the elders, and the elders to the Prophets, and the Prophets committed it to the men of the Great Synagogue."[7] From this perspective, it can be said that the Christian and the Jewish oral traditions are strictly analogous phenomena.

However, between the Gospel tradition and the scribal tradition there is a great difference that goes back to the words of Jesus themselves. The words of Jesus are inseparable from His person, whereas the scribes stood apart from their teachings, which were considered to be greater than their persons. The scribes were vehicles of tradition, and they attached disciples not so much to themselves as to the tradition they taught. Jesus' words are different. The saying in Mark 8:38, "Whoever is ashamed of me and of my words," shows that Jesus' words are inseparable from His person. He is Himself present in His words. The words of Jesus were not like the words of the scribes; the difference impressed itself at once upon the people (Mark 1:22). The scribes were simply conveyors of tradition. A praiseworthy scribe was "a plastered cistern which loseth not a drop" of the traditions of the elders,[8] but faithfully preserves and teaches it to the next generations. Although many similarities may be noted between the teachings of Jesus and the scribes, they belonged to two different religious worlds. The scribes taught

[7] See Aboth 1:1 in *The Mishnah*, Herbert Danby, ed. (Oxford: Clarendon, 1933), p. 446.
[8] Pirke Aboth 2:10.

and nothing happened. Jesus spoke, and demons fled, storms were settled (Mark 4:39), dead were raised (Mark 5:41). Jesus' words were not merely a tradition, a teaching, an instruction; they embodied authority and power — the authority of His own person in whom the Kingdom of God was present.[9]

The same "transcendent" dimension found in the words of Jesus is found in the Gospel tradition. It is not simply a human tradition to instruct the ignorant; it is itself the Word of God. This fact illustrates again what is inescapable in biblical study: that criticism and theology cannot be isolated from each other. As the person of Jesus imparted authority to His words, so the Holy Spirit imparted authority to the Gospel tradition.

Evangelical Christians often overlook the important fact that the many references to the Word of God in the New Testament are not to the written books of the Bible but to the oral tradition before it assumed written form. The preaching of Jesus is regarded as the Word of God (Luke 5:1; 8:11; 8:21; 11:28), for the Word of Jesus is itself the Word of God (John 14:24). The Word preached by the apostles in the early church is the Word of God (Acts 4:29; 6:2; 8:14; 8:25); so is the gospel preached by Paul (Acts 13:5; 13:46; 16:32). Paul frequently refers to the gospel he had preached as the Word of God (I Cor. 14:36; II Cor. 2:17; 4:2; Phil. 1:14; Col. 1:25; see Col. 1:5, where the "word of truth" is the gospel). The widely quoted verse, "For the word of God is living and active, sharper than any two-edged sword" (Heb. 4:12) does not refer to the written New Testament, for it had not yet been compiled, nor does it designate the Old Testament. The Word of God is the gospel of Jesus preserved at first largely in oral form. This is proved by Hebrews 13:7: "Remember your leaders, those who spoke to you the word of God." This gospel is "the commandment of the Lord and Saviour given through your apostles" (II Pet. 3:2) and superintended by the Holy Spirit (I Pet. 1:12).

The all-important fact is that the Word of God was preserved

9 See W. Foerster, in *Theological Dictionary of the New Testament*, trans. by G. W. Bromiley (Grand Rapids: Eerdmans, 1964), II, 566.

in the church by the apostles in oral form, and was superintended by the Holy Spirit before it assumed written form. We
may conclude, therefore, that the contention of form criticism
that the Gospel tradition was preserved in oral form for a generation by the church is not only a fact which is attested strongly
by the New Testament, but is also a fact of great theological
importance. Not only was the Holy Spirit active in the writing
of the books of the New Testament; he was also active in the
history of the Gospel tradition before it assumed written form.
This theological fact is seldom recognized by form critics, for
they usually work as historians, not as theologians.

A second valid contention of form criticism is that the Gospels are not "neutral, objective, impartial" records but are
witnesses to the faith of Christian believers. This point is often
misunderstood, and great care must be taken to define terms
correctly.

What is an "objective" report? This word can have two
meanings: it can refer to a record of events as they actually happened; or it can designate a record composed by authors who
do not take sides, who are "open-minded" in the sense that they
are uncommitted, who are neutral in the sense that they are
themselves indifferent toward the material they record.

This question of "objectivity" is frequently misunderstood
from two opposite directions. Some scholars feel that a committed author cannot be truly open-minded and objective, but
that his very commitment will of necessity lead him unconsciously to distort the actual facts in favor of his commitment. From
this point of view, only an unbeliever could write a truly historical record; only a non-Christian would be capable of describing "what really happened"; any Christian account must be so
colored by faith that facts are swallowed up or largely distorted
by faith.

On the other hand, evangelicals sometimes take the position
that objectivity implies objective facts whose full significance is
self-evident to all observers apart from any exercise of faith. If
Jesus was the incarnate Son of God, objectively considered, this

fact must have been so obvious in the person, deeds and words of Jesus as to be clearly recognizable to all observers. If Jesus was actually divine, no faith should be necessary to recognize it; it should be a fact which forces itself upon all observers.

We would suggest that the best solution of this very difficult problem lies between the two extremes: the redemptive events recorded in the Gospels are "objective" in the sense that they really happened in time and space, but their nature is such that they stand apart from merely human "historical" events, even though they occurred in history, for they cannot be understood by ordinary human observation but only by the response of faith.

The problem can be described in another way. If men had been responsive to the Word of God, they would have recognized and understood what God was doing in these redemptive events. But unbelief blinded them to the real meaning of the events unfolding before their eyes. This does not mean that faith read something into the historical event which was not there; it means rather that only faith could apprehend the real redemptive significance of the person and mission of Jesus.

The experience of Paul illustrates this fact. Paul's faith did not change the human Jesus into a divine redeemer. On the contrary, faith enabled Paul to understand who Jesus really was. Before his conversion, Paul (then Saul of Tarsus) interpreted Christ "according to the flesh" (II Cor. 5:16), i.e., by human, unbelieving standards. Jesus was interpreted as a Jewish prophet who had claimed to be Messiah, but whose claim was obviously false; for according to the Jewish understanding of the Old Testament, based on such prophecies as Isaiah 9 and 11, the Messiah's essential role was to reign and subdue all enemies of God (and Israel). For the unbelieving Jewish rabbi, Saul, the fact that Jesus was crucified by pagan hands proved that He could not be what He claimed. Interpreted by human standards, "according to the flesh," Jesus was a pretender who deserved to be executed for His blasphemous claims. But when Paul came to faith and interpreted Christ "according to the Spirit," he saw

Him for what He really was — not only Messiah, but also the incarnate Son of God.

This interpretation we believe is demanded by the Scripture itself. Jesus' Messiahship as the Son of God was not a self-evident fact. "Flesh and blood," the merely human level of knowledge and understanding, did not reveal this fact to Peter, but only the heavenly Father (Matt. 16:17). The truth of the gospel is hidden from the wise and understanding but revealed by God to those who have childlike faith (Matt. 11:25). Those who have such faith can understand the mysteries of the Kingdom of God which are enigmatic to those who do not believe (Matt. 13:11ff.).

The fact is that a nonbeliever could not write a gospel. A gospel is good news about what God has done in Jesus; an unbeliever would only describe the wonderful — or bewildering — words and deeds of a remarkable Jewish teacher.

We have a number of incidents in the New Testament reflecting such unbelieving "objectivity." Confronted by Jesus' mighty works, the Pharisees admitted that He had more than human power, but they claimed that He was in league with the devil (Matt. 12:24). His own closest friends — those who knew Him within the intimacy of the family circle — thought He was out of His head (Mark 3:21).

The much debated statement of Paul in II Corinthians 5:16 illustrates this problem. "From now on, therefore, we regard no one 'according to the flesh'; even though we once regarded Christ 'according to the flesh,' we regard him thus no longer." This verse designates two ways of looking at life: from the perspective of human judgments, and from the perspective of Christian faith.

Saul, the Jewish rabbi, viewed Jesus as other Jews interpreted Him: as a false messianic pretender who blasphemously had claimed to be the Son of God but whose claims had been nailed to a Roman cross. To appreciate this, we must recall that the Jews did not understand Isaiah 53 to have anything to do with the Messiah. Contemporary Jewish literature proves that the Jews believed that the Messiah would be the conquering Davidic King predicted in Isaiah 9 and 11. It is noteworthy that Isaiah 53 does not attribute redeeming sufferings to *Messiah* but to an undesignated Servant of the Lord. The Jews understood this servant to be the people Israel; and for this interpretation they could claim the authority of Isaiah himself (Isa. 41:8; 43:1-10; 44:1, 2, 21; 45:4; 49:3). The role of Messiah was not to die at the hands of wicked men, but to destroy all evildoers and to reign in righteousness over His redeemed people (Isaiah 11:4-5). Furthermore, Scripture itself asserted that death on a tree involved a curse (Gal. 3:13).

This is why the cross was a stumbling block to the Jews (I Cor. 1:23), for it seemed to contradict the Word of God itself. This explains why even those who had been with Jesus throughout His ministry, who had seen His deeds, heard His words, sensed His divine person, and even heard predictions of impending death, lost hope when He died (Luke 24:21). In spite of all that Jesus was and did and said, it was only His resurrection and His appearances afterward that created renewed faith in His person and in the reality of God's redemptive presence in Him. Apart from the resurrection, there never would have been a gospel, either oral or written. Unbelief cannot write such a gospel. The gospel is the good news of what God has done in Jesus; but unbelief cannot talk about God's redemptive acts in history. An unbeliever can describe Jesus as an unusual man possessing demonic power, a madman, a trickster, a man of magnetic personality, a paragon of virtue, the ethical ideal of mankind, a man perfectly dedicated to God, a man open to the future. It cannot describe Him as the incarnate Son of God. This is the language of faith, even though the event itself involved full objectivity.

The admission that only faith could write a gospel does not necessitate the conclusion that such faith cannot be "objective," and that it results inevitably in a distortion of the facts in its own interests. On the contrary, only faith can really recognize what the facts really were. The New Testament bears witness that the disciples did not truly understand who Jesus was until after the resurrection. Only as they looked back to what Jesus had said and done, viewing His person and deeds and words in the light of their resurrection faith, and saw that He was indeed the "Son of God in power" (Rom. 1:4), could they correctly understand why He had acted as He had.[10]

At this point form criticism has made a substantial contribution to an evangelical understanding of the Gospels in a negative way. *Form criticism has failed to discover a purely historical Jesus.* Wrede, in contrast to the old liberal interpreters of Jesus as an ethical prophet, recognized correctly that the Jesus portrayed in Mark is no mere teacher of love and righteousness but a divine Messiah. However, since a divine Messiah cannot be historical, Wrede invented the famous theory of the "Messianic Secret." He held that Jesus made no claim to be Messiah and had no messianic mission. Only the resurrection created belief in Jesus' Messiahship. After the resurrection, the church read Messiahship back into the life of Jesus. Yet the church was embarrassed by the fact that the historical tradition about Jesus was non-messianic, and therefore in effect contradicted their faith in His Messiahship. How did the church relieve this embarrassment of possessing a non-messianic tradition while it held a messianic faith? By inventing the idea of the Messianic Secret. Jesus was Messiah and knew Himself to be such; but His disciples did not know it because He kept it from them. It was His secret which He did not disclose until after the resurrection. This Messianic Secret, which appears in the Gospel of Mark in such passages as 1:34; 8:30; 9:9, is not historical, i.e., it does not reflect what happened. It is rather a literary device created by the believing church and read into the tradition to solve the church's dilemma, created by a non-messianic tradition. Mark changes the non-messianic tradition into a hidden messianic tradition.

While this theory is still supported by some contemporary

[10] See Bo Reicke, "Incarnation and Exaltation," *Interpretation,* 16 (1962), pp. 156-68.

critics, most notably by Rudolf Bultmann and his followers, it has not commended itself to a more sober and cautious criticism. The fact is that *we do not have a non-messianic tradition.* Such a "neutral" tradition is a purely hypothetical critical reconstruction, which rests on rather flimsy evidence. A recent British critic speaks of the "Wrede Avenue" which leads nowhere.[11]

When a critic is open to the consistent evidence not only of the Gospels but of the entire New Testament, he finds that instead of a Messianic Secret, the modern scholars are faced with *The Riddle of the New Testament,*[12] which is Jesus Christ Himself. The several New Testament documents do not reflect a process of transformation of the man, Jesus of Nazareth, into the divine Christ. "No deifying of a prophet or of a mere preacher of righteousness can be detected." There is no literary evidence that a period ever existed when Jesus was viewed as a purely "historical" figure, that is, as only a man, or that such a historical figure was later transformed by theological reinterpretation. The fact is that the historian must admit that all of the New Testament documents, with all of their diversity, reflect a real unity at one point: that Jesus bears a transcendent significance which "history" cannot account for.

This means, in theological idiom, that all of the New Testament documents view Christ as a divine person, the Son of God. Form criticism has tried to reconstruct the various stages in the alleged development of Christology; but it has found no documentary witness for a non-divine Jesus. The purely "historical Jesus" is a hypothesis of a modern criticism that derives its presuppositions from modern philosophies, not from the biblical accounts. The consistent witness of the New Testament is that in the person of Jesus of Nazareth, God Himself has entered into history for man's salvation. This is a "riddle" for

11 T. W. Manson, "Present-day Research in the Life of Jesus," in *The Background of the New Testament and its Eschatology,* W. D. Davies and D. Daube, eds. (Cambridge: University Press, 1956), p. 216.

12 See the book of this title by E. C. Hoskyns and Noel Davey (London: Faber and Faber, 1931).

the modern historian. As a recent writer has said, "History can go so far as to define the riddle, to formulate precisely the terms in which it presents itself to the human race; but it remains a riddle of the Sphinx until another dimension than that of history is called in to aid in its resolution."[13] This added dimension is faith. The Gospels were written from the perspective of faith, and must be accepted in faith, in addition to being studied by the techniques of historical criticism.

We agree heartily, therefore, with the form critics that the Gospels are not "neutral, objective" records but are the product of Christian faith; but we must further assert that this fact in no way renders the Gospels untrustworthy. On the contrary, we must insist that only a historical criticism which is tempered by faith can really recognize what God has done in history in Jesus of Nazareth. By the nature of the problem, criticism cannot prove the truthfulness of the Gospels, for at the heart of the Gospels is the gospel: the acting of God in and through historical events; and history by definition deals only with human conduct and relationships, not with the acts of God.

By the same token, if the supernatural really occurred in history, criticism cannot disprove it. Its naturalistic presuppositions require that it interpret the supernatural as legend, mythology. It is of considerable significance that criticism has not found objective, documentary, historical evidence to establish the existence of a non-supernatural Jesus. The very existence of a purely "historical Jesus" is a critical hypothesis. The evidence supports the claim that Jesus was a supernatural person, even though the historian as historian cannot confess it. Such a confession is possible only to faith.

We shall now examine a third thesis of form criticism, namely, that the material in the Gospels must be studied in terms of its *Sitz im Leben* — its life setting in the early church.

It should be obvious, upon reflection, that this is, to a certain extent, a valid position. Our four Gospels present a unified

---

[13] Stephen Neill, *The Interpretation of the New Testament 1861-1961*, (New York: Oxford, 1964), p. 218.

witness to the essential person of Jesus, but they have different emphases. How are these differences to be explained?

Mark's main interest is the person of Jesus and His conflict with the scribes and Pharisees. His chief purpose is to explain who this Jesus was whom the church now recognizes as her resurrected and exalted Lord, and how it happened that He was put to death on a Roman cross. Matthew is concerned with questions which troubled the minds of Jewish Christians. If the Jews rejected Jesus and turned Him over to Rome to be crucified, could He really be the messianic King promised in the Old Testament? And if the destruction of the Jewish state in A.D. 66-70 was God's judgment on Israel for rejecting her messianic King, what element of continuity exists between Israel and the church? What should be the Christian's attitude toward the law? In answering such questions for a Jewish-Christian community, Matthew enlarges Mark by adding large blocks of teaching material, in particular dealing with the law, Christian conduct, and the church. Luke views the life of Jesus in its setting in the larger scene of world history, and in its relationship to the time of the church. This particular emphasis of the Third Gospel is shown by the specific chronological reference in chapter 3:1, and in the fact that the Gospel is only the first half of the single continuous two-volume narrative, Luke-Acts. In a sense, the Gospel serves as an introduction to the book of Acts which tells the story of the church: how it began as a small Jewish sect in Jerusalem and finally became a Gentile community in the capital city of the Roman Empire. Luke sees the answer in the mission of Jesus itself, which is interpreted as an event of universal importance in world history. John's Gospel was written to expound the divine nature of the Messiah in the specific interests of saving faith (John 20:31). The Fourth Gospel places great emphasis upon the deity of Christ and the reality of His incarnation, drawing upon the author's own memory of Jesus and his own understanding of the tradition about Him to write a Gospel quite different from the first three.

It is quite legitimate to try to ascertain the historical situation in the first-century churches which would have led to the writing of four such different Gospels although it must be recognized that such study is highly hypothetical. It makes good historical sense to conclude, as tradition says, that Mark was written in Rome to explain to a largely Gentile audience how it happened that, if Jesus was indeed the Son of God and Messiah, He was rejected by the leaders of the Jewish nation and executed on a Roman cross. It is also historically very plausible to conclude that Matthew was written for a Jewish Christian community, possibly in Antioch of Syria, to show that Jesus as the King of Israel was the fulfillment of the Old Testament prophecies, that although Israel rejected her Messiah, Jesus brought into being a new people of God, for whom the Old Testament law as reinterpreted by Jesus and fulfilled in His person and mission possessed an abiding validity. A similar search must be carried out for the historical setting of Luke and John.

The problem in finding the historical setting of the Fourth Gospel is particularly difficult, because John's idiom is different from that of the first three Gospels. The latter have much to say about the Kingdom of God, which is a thoroughly Jewish concept quite at home in first-century Palestine, but John records Jesus as talking about the world above and below as the realms of light and darkness. Jesus came from the realm of light into the world of darkness to bring men the light of life (John 1:4-5; 8:12; 12:46). This is quite a different emphasis from that found in the Synoptic Gospels. Since similar ideas are to be found in Greek religious writings, especially in a collection of writings known as the Hermetic literature, it was long a common practice for scholars to conclude that John's Gospel reflects a *Sitz im Leben* in the Hellenistic world, and embodies a radical reinterpretation of the person and message of Jesus in non-Jewish terms. It has been widely maintained, therefore, that this Gospel has very little historical value in preserving the actual message of Jesus.

This position, which had become almost a critical dogma,

was shaken by the discovery since 1947 of the literature of the Jewish sect known as the Qumran community, which lived as a separatist colony near the Dead Sea. This literature, like the Fourth Gospel, contains a thought pattern of two realms of light and darkness. Its terminology is strikingly similar to that of John. This does not mean that either Jesus or John was a member of this colony; but it does establish a revolutionary fact of criticism, namely, that the idiom of the Fourth Gospel was at home in early first-century Palestine. This conclusion has introduced a new day for Johannine studies as scholars are compelled to re-evaluate their former theories about the *Sitz im Leben* of John. Some have even argued that John may have been the earliest written Gospel. A former president of the world's most learned society of New Testament scholars published a paper defending the thesis that John was written to prove to Hellenistic Jews[14] that Jesus was indeed their Messiah, as the Gospel itself claims (John 20:31).

But though we readily admit that each Gospel must be studied in terms of its supposed *Sitz im Leben,* it does not follow that this *Sitz im Leben* exercised a significant creative factor in the formation of the content of the Gospel tradition. The most recent development within the form critical school is the so-called *Redaktionstheologie.* The older application of the documentary sources hypothesis viewed the Evangelists more or less as scissors-and-paste editors, not creative authors, who artificially compiled material from their diverse literary sources, with little reference to the historical facts. *Redaktionstheologie* views the Evangelists as genuine creative authors, each of whom has distinctive theological views which are expressed in the Gospels. However, the Gospels represent the theology of their authors and of the communities in which they were produced rather than the teachings of the historical Jesus. History is swallowed up by theology.

There can be little doubt that the needs of a given community

---

14 Hellenistic Jews are those who lived outside of Palestine, scattered throughout the Graeco-Roman world.

contributed to the selection of material included in each Gospel, for it should be obvious that our Gospels record only a small fragment of the actual deeds and words of Jesus. However, the view that the Gospels do not preserve authentic traditions but embody to a considerable degree material created by the communities overlooks four important facts: (1) the brief period of time which elapsed between the events and the record of the events, (2) the role of eyewitnesses in preserving the tradition, (3) the role of the authoritative apostolic witness, and (4) the role of the Holy Spirit. As Vincent Taylor has vividly expressed it, the view of the extreme form critics practically assumes that all eyewitnesses were taken out of the church at the time of the ascension of the Lord.[15] However, Luke (1:1-2) asserts the role of eyewitnesses and of "ministers of the word" — probably apostles — in the transmission of the tradition. Harald Riesenfeld may go too far in denying the role of preaching and teaching in the preservation of the Gospel tradition, but he is certainly right in his view that the early church preserved the Gospel tradition not only because it was useful, but also because of an interest in Jesus Himself.[16]

In dealing with the question of the *Sitz im Leben* of the Gospels, form critics have established a critical principle which seems highly arbitrary. This is the principle that only those passages in the Gospels can be accepted as historically trustworthy which have no parallel either in the early church or contemporary Judaism.[17] Any passages in the Gospels which have parallels in either the early church or in Judaism may reflect Christian or Jewish thought, not that of Jesus Himself. The positive force of this principle cannot be avoided; but it un-

---

[15] Vincent Taylor, *The Formation of the Gospel Tradition* (London: Macmillan, 1933), pp. 41ff.

[16] "The Gospel Tradition and its Beginnings," *Studia Evangelica* (K. Aland, *et al.*, eds. [Berlin: Akademie Verlag, 1959]), pp. 43-64; C. F. D. Moule, "The Intention of the Evangelists," *New Testament Essays* (A. J. B. Higgins, ed. [Manchester: University Press, 1959]), pp. 165-79.

[17] E. Käsemann, *Essays on New Testament Themes* (Naperville: Allenson, 1964), p. 44. For a very different critical norm of authenticity see Oscar Cullmann, *Heil als Geschichte* (Tübingen: Mohr, 1965), pp. 172f.

necessarily restricts the basis of authenticity. Would we not expect that there would be parallels between Jesus' teaching and His Jewish environment? After all, He was a first-century Jew. Would we not expect His teachings to be useful in the church? This critical norm has, as a recent reviewer well pointed out, decided in advance that the result will be: "a Jesus who was unorthodox, since anything that savours of orthodoxy, Jewish or Christian, has been excluded *a priori*."[18]

Therefore, we may conclude that while we must try to reconstruct the *Sitz im Leben* of each Gospel to determine why its life setting led to the particular choice and arrangement of materials, and even to what degree the *Sitz im Leben* modified the form in which the tradition was preserved, we must demur at the conclusions of extreme form critics that the church played a significant creative role in preserving the traditions. As Stephen Neill has pointed out, this would mean that the anonymous community had far greater creative power than Jesus of Nazareth, although faith in Him had called the church into being.[19]

We must yet examine the claim of form criticism that all the geographical and temporal references in the Gospels which provide the framework for the life of Jesus are later inventions of the Evangelists and quite unhistorical. The many single units of tradition are thought to have existed independently without historical setting, and later to have been strung together by the Evangelists and placed in an artificial and unhistorical framework of the "life of Christ."

This problem must be discussed first of all in light of the data in the Gospels themselves. What does an analysis of the Gospel structure suggest about the nature of the tradition? Let us examine the early chapters of Mark.

The first chapter of Mark ties several units of material together with specific references to the time and place. Jesus was

18 A. T. Hanson in *Scottish Journal of Theology,* 18 (1965), p. 107.
19 Stephen Neill, *The Interpretation of the New Testament 1861-1961* (London: Oxford, 1964), p. 250.

in Capernaum on a Sabbath (Mark 1:21). "That evening" (1:32) He performed miracles. "In the morning" (1:35) He went out of the city. Mark concludes this "day in Capernaum" with a summary statement: "He went throughout all Galilee, preaching in their synagogues and casting out demons" (1:39). We must ask the question: Where did He go? What cities did He visit? What was His itinerary? How long did it last? Did any notable events occur? What did His ministry accomplish? The answer: silence. Mark does not say. He inserts a single incident about a leper (1:40-45) but does not say when it happened. Then Jesus returned to Capernaum (2:1), where He performed a miracle of healing and forgiveness recorded by Mark (2:2-12). What else happened? How long did Jesus stay in Capernaum? The answer: silence. "He went out again beside the sea" (2:13). When? What happened there besides the call of Levi? "And as he sat at table in his house" (2:15); but did He return to Capernaum immediately after the call of Levi by the sea? If so, how long did He stay in Capernaum? What other events occurred? Mark does not say. Instead, he adds three incidents: about fasting, about plucking corn on a Sabbath, about healing on a Sabbath in the synagogue (2:18-22; 2:23-28; 3:1-6). However, these are not related chronologically or geographically to what precedes. "One sabbath he was going through the grainfields" (2:23). When? Where? Why? "Again he entered the synagogue" (3:1). When? Where? Why? Obviously, such events are selected and narrated because they belong together topically and serve Mark's purpose of showing the beginnings of conflict between Jesus and the Pharisees, not because of their chronological relatedness.

Such a survey makes it quite clear that in his Gospel Mark is not trying to write a chronicle of continuous events, or a "biography," or a travel narrative. He is giving a series of events which he deliberately strings together rather loosely. Throughout the Gospel of Mark the introductory words to each paragraph make it obvious that this is Mark's prevailing method.

Therefore it appears to be true, based on the Gospel's witness to itself, that many of these incidents were preserved orally as detached incidents. If, as tradition says, Mark embodies the re- miniscences of Peter in Rome, is this not what we would ex- pect? Authentic memory functions in this way. It can remem- ber broad outlines; it can remember many single incidents; it can at times recall certain sequences. This is, in fact, what we find in Mark. It is very likely (and here we are dealing with historical probabilities, based on a survey of the Gospel itself) that Peter in his preaching and teaching used many events from the life of Jesus, which he vividly and accurately remembered, to illustrate Jesus' message and mission. The important thing is not the order or sequence of events; it is rather who Jesus was and how it came about that the Son of God was crucified. Therefore, it does no damage to the Gospel to admit the pos- sibility of a large measure of truth in form criticism's under- standing of the nature of the traditions. The Gospel supports such a claim.

This conclusion is reinforced by Matthew's rearrangement of the events recorded in the first part of Mark's Gospel. Be- fore the Sermon on the Mount, Matthew writes only three of the events recorded in Mark: the journey to Galilee (Matt. 4:12-17 = Mark 1:14-15), the call of the disciples (Matt. 4:18- 22 = Mark 1:16-20), and a preaching tour in Galilee (Matt. 4:23-25 = Mark 1:39). Other events he transposes: the healing of Peter's mother-in-law (Mark 1:29-31 = Matt. 8:14-15), the healing of the sick (Mark 1:32-34 = Matt. 8:16-17). Still other events he omits: the healing and forgiveness in the synagogue (Mark 1:21-28) and the departure from Capernaum (Mark 1: 35-38).

Matthew's rearrangement of Mark's order of events continues through chapters 8-10; chapter 11 contains materials lacking in Mark which Matthew shares with Luke, but in different order. However, after chapter 12, Matthew follows Mark's order of events, with the exception of three incidents in Mark 4:35-5:43, which Matthew has already related in chapters 8-9. Most of these chronological transpositions are made without hard and fast chronological or geographical notes. In other words, Matthew deliberately rearranges Mark's order of events, not because he thought they were historically wrong and he wishes to correct Mark's errors, but because a topical rearrangement better suited Matthew's purpose. A failure to recognize fully that the Evangelists obviously had no biographical concerns will result in attributing to them alleged historical errors that are in reality no part of their purpose and should not therefore be seen as errors at all.

The conclusion that the Gospels are in part topical arrangements of material which was preserved in distinct units appears also in the recorded teachings of Jesus. All three Gospels record a day of parables (Mark 4, Matt. 13, Luke 8), but do not agree in the parables spoken on this occasion. Mark ends the collection with the parable of the mustard seed (Mark 4:30-32) and then gives a summarizing conclusion (Mark. 4:33-34). Matthew (but not Luke) follows Mark at this point; but Matthew inserts another parable — that of the leaven, which Luke records in a very different context (Matt. 13:33 = Luke 13:20-21). Then, with a shift of locale, Matthew adds the explanation of the parable of the wheat and the weeds (Matt. 13:36-43), to which are attached without editorial comment the parables of the treasure, pearl, and dragnet (13:44-50). All of this is capped by a final Matthean summary (13:51-52). These facts suggest that Matthew has used the occasion of Mark's account of the parables to add several other parables dealing with the same theme of the Kingdom of God. Matthew may have been familiar with these parables as they were preserved in the Gospel tradition as independent units.

The same phenomenon of diversity of arrangement is quite clear in Matthew's and Luke's account of the Sermon on the Mount. Matthew (5-8) and Luke (6:17-49) have the same beginning, and most of Luke's sermon is contained in Matthew's account, but Matthew's account of the sermon is over three times as long as Luke's, and much of his material is found elsewhere in Luke's Gospel, sometimes practically word for word (cf. Matt. 6:22-23 = Luke 11:34-35; Matt. 6:24 = Luke 16:13; Matt. 6:25-33 = Luke 12:22-31). The conclusion is inescapable that Matthew and Luke deliberately arrange their materials not in terms of how they think the events they record happened historically, but in terms of the portrait of Jesus' person, mission, and message they wish to sketch. This may well be due to the fact that many of the sayings of Jesus were preserved as independent units and were arranged by the Evangelists to suit their purposes.

We must insist that it is poor criticism to demand biographical precision of the Evangelists when they themselves obviously did not intend it. This does not mean that we can go all the way with the form critics. Their conclusion that we have no trustworthy historical outline for the life of Jesus does not follow. That Jesus' mission was preceded by that of John the Baptist, that it was opened by His baptism and temptation, that there was a Galilean ministry, a great sermon, a day of parables, that conflict with the scribes and Pharisees arose early, that the understanding of the disciples came to a great climax with Peter's confession (Mark 8), followed by announcements of Jesus' impending death, that Jesus finally journeyed to Jerusalem, cleansed the temple, engaged in a last sacred meal with His disciples, was betrayed, tried, and crucified — all of this may be accepted as trustworthy history. The eyewitnesses in the formative years of the Gospel tradition would not likely forget such important events as these. In fact, it has been effectively argued by critical scholars that a broad outline of the life of Jesus was handed down as part of the tradition.[20] That within this broad historical outline each Evangelist arranged his material to serve his own purpose is no criticism of the historicity and authenticity of this material, unless the critic forces upon the material standards which were no part of the Evangelists' purpose.

We may conclude this discussion by recognizing that in spite of its excesses, form criticism has thrown considerable light on

[20] See C. H. Dodd, "The Framework of the Gospel Narrative," *Expository Times*, 43 (1932), pp. 396ff.

the nature of the Gospels and the traditions they employ. Evangelical scholars should be willing to accept this light. However, the extreme form critics are controlled by presuppositions which are alien to the New Testament texts themselves,[21] and which not only fall far short of proof or even of historical probability, but which are incapable of solving the most difficult problem raised by the method itself: the problem of the uniqueness of the person of Jesus Christ.

21 See below, chapter VIII, "Comparative Religions Criticism."

CHAPTER VII

Historical Criticism

THE RELIGIOUS FAITH AND PRACTICE OF ISRAEL DID NOT ARISE IN A vacuum, but in the cultural setting of ancient Semitic religions. In the same way, the early church arose against the background of first-century Judaism and the Hellenistic world. An adequate understanding of the biblical message demands a familiarity with these religious environments.

It is self-evident that any word, concept, or document must be interpreted in its own historical setting. For example, the word "evangelical" as it is used in this book denotes American Protestant Christians who hold a "high" view of the Bible. The equivalent in German, *"evangelisch,"* means Protestant, in contrast to *katholisch* (Catholic). Again, the American use of the word "church" may refer to a denomination or a local congregation, Protestant or Catholic. The German *"Kirche"* designates only established state churches, Protestant or Catholic. The so-called "free" Baptist churches in Germany do not call themselves *"Kirchen,"* but *"Gemeinden"* (fellowships), to distinguish themselves from the state churches.

A word, concept, or document is often misleading unless it

171

is interpreted within its historical setting. Paul's discussion of the problem of meats offered to idols (Rom. 14; I Cor. 8) has no relevance at all unless it is seen in its context. His assertion, "One believes he may eat anything, while the weak man eats only vegetables" (Rom. 14:2), has nothing to do with the merits of a vegetarian diet, as one might be led to believe if he were unacquainted with the background. This statement deals with the problem raised for Christians by the fact that most meat sold in the open market had come from pagan temples where it had first been sacrificed to an idol and then turned over to the meat market for public sale. How should a Christian who had been delivered from pagan worship view such meat which had been devoted to an idol? By eating it, did he not compromise his Christian faith? Did he not tacitly approve of pagan worship by buying such meat? Was the meat itself not rendered unclean by its use in heathen worship? Should not a Christian who desired complete separation from the world of pagan practice and worship draw the line at meat which was associated with idol worship? Would not the money spent on such meat help support the temple system?

Paul's answer again is meaningless in a modern context: "Eat what ever is sold in the meat market (μάκελλον) without raising any question on the ground of conscience" (I Cor. 10: 25). Furthermore, Paul says that if a believer is inclined to accept an invitation from a pagan friend to have dinner with him, he is to eat whatever is set before him without interrogating his host as to whether the meat served him had been sacrificed in a pagan temple the day before. Probably no reader of this book has ever been faced with this problem. But one who has visited the ruins at Pompeii can understand the significance of Paul's words. Surrounding the Forum are the temples of the deities worshipped by the citizens, and in one corner adjacent to the temples are the ruins of the Macellum with its row of small shops where the carcasses of the slain animals were brought from the surrounding temples to be sold to the residents of the city for food. Might not the pagan neighbor of a recent convert to Christ, seeing him buy meat in the Macellum, assume that he had just come from a temple feast? Should a believer not insist on complete "separation from the world," including avoidance of such meats?

Paul's answer is forthright. Pagan idols are no-gods; there is one God who is the creator of all flesh; and God gave animal flesh as food for men. Therefore the mature, "strong" believer recognizes that no flesh can be ceremonially unclean, and there is no merit in abstinence, for "the earth is the Lord's and everything in it" (I Cor. 10:26) and "everything is indeed clean" (Rom. 14:20), and is to be received with thanksgiving. However, not all believers are mature enough to understand this truth. Some have weak consciences and have not grasped the meaning of Christian freedom. Therefore the strong believers should not exercise their liberty in such a way as to offend their weaker brothers and cause them to stumble and relapse into pagan worship; but by the same token, the weak believer with a sensitive conscience should not sit in judgment on his brother who does not share his scruples. The prevailing rule must be Christian love and consideration.

This particular historical problem does not have application to the modern Western world (it is still a problem in parts of Asia), but the principles involved have a permanent validity. In various cultural situations, certain practices are considered quite innocent by devout believers but are offensive to others. In such matters, the two biblical principles of freedom and loving consideration ought to prevail. The essential principles embodied in the ancient historical situation have permanent validity, even though the particular historical problem has passed away with the ancient world.

This type of criticism, known as historical criticism, may affect the interpretation of profound theological questions. One of the most vivid and relevant illustrations of the necessity of such historical criticism is the problem of the terminology used in the Gospels to designate the person of our Lord. The three most important terms are "Son of God," "Son of Man," and

"Messiah." A prevalent unhistorical theological interpretation of these three terms identifies "Messiah" with "Son of God," and views the two expressions "Son of God" and "Son of Man" as presenting the deity and humanity of the God-man. One of the first exponents of this explanation was Ignatius of Antioch, in the second century after Christ (*Ad Eph.* 2.20). Ignatius' explanation, however, represents an interpretation in Greek rather than Jewish categories. Since Jesus was a Jew addressing a message to Jews, a historical interpretation of these three names requires an investigation of what they would convey to a Jewish audience.

The Old Testament use of "Messiah" hardly ever designates the divinely sent redeemer. The understanding of "Messiah" in first-century Judaism was that portrayed in the Psalms of Solomon (first century B.C.), in which the Messiah is seen as a divinely endowed Jewish king empowered by God to defeat the hated Romans, destroy the enemies of Israel (and God), deliver Jerusalem from military oppression, and establish an effective political and religious sovereignty over the world. The Kingdom of God meant to the Jews the kingdom of Israel. It was in this light that such prophecies as Isaiah 9 and 11 were seen.

The Fourth Evangelist reports that the feeding of the five thousand showed Jesus to be endowed with divine power (John 6:15). His message was the coming of the Kingdom of God (Mark 1:14), and the Jewish people, identifying the Kingdom of God with the kingdom of Israel, tried to force His hand by crowning Him king and making Him assume what they understood as the rôle of the Messiah, the political and military deliverer and conqueror. When Jesus made it clear that His messianic rôle was a spiritual deliverance, not a political one, "many of his disciples drew back and no longer went about with him" (John 6:66). Matthew's form of the report of Peter's confession is a result of the fact that the disciples had begun to understand that Jesus was indeed the expected Messiah, but of a different order than that anticipated by the popular understanding. Jesus was the Messiah who is also the Son of God (Matt. 16:16).

This raises a further question which both historical criticism and exegesis must answer. What content is conveyed by the term "Son of God"? This may not seem to be relevant to an uncritical reader of the Gospels. "Son of God" obviously designates God the Son, the second person of the trinity. There are indeed passages in the Bible which clearly teach the deity of Christ (John 1:1; Phil. 2:6; Rom. 9:5 [RSV^mg]; Col. 1:19; Titus 2:13; Matt. 28: 19); but this should not lead to the easy conclusion that the title "Son of God" designates this deity.

As a matter of fact, "Son of God" has numerous meanings in the Bible. The angels are called "sons of God" (Job 1:6; 2:1). The nation Israel is God's son, his firstborn (Ex. 4:22). Adam is God's son (Luke 3:38). "Son of God" can designate anyone whose existence is due to the immediate creative activity of God. Paul states that all men are God's offspring (Acts 17:28) in the sense that mankind owes its very existence to one God. There is a biblical doctrine of the universal fatherhood of God; but this fatherhood is a creative relationship, not a redemptive one. It is in this sense that Jesus Himself is called "Son of God" in Luke 1:35; His birth is due to a direct creative act of God the Holy Spirit, not to ordinary human procreation.

"Son of God" can also be used to designate an intimate spiritual relationship. This is the deeper meaning of Exodus 4:22. The people of Israel not only owed their existence to an act of God in history; Israel was also God's firstborn, the special object of God's fatherly love. Throughout the Old Testament, the particular relationship of Israel to God is described in terms of sonship (Deut. 14:1; Jer. 31:9, 20; Hos. 11:1); and in the New Testament this term is used to describe the new intimate relationship which followers of Jesus Christ have towards God; they *become* sons of God in a new and vital sense (Rom. 8:14, 19; Gal. 3:26; 4:5).

A difficult historical problem is whether "Son of God" was ever used in Judaism as a designation for the Messiah. There are indications in the Old Testament that the promised Davidic King would be called God's son because He would be the special object of God's care (II Sam. 7:14; Psalm 89:27, 29). In Psalm 2:7, God says to His anointed King, "you are my son, today I have begotten you." The promised King-deliverer, by virtue of His messianic office, is called God's son. In the New Testament, this verse is used in at least one place to designate the exalted status of the resurrected Lord who is enthroned at the right hand of God (Acts 13:33). Although He was the Son of God on earth, His exaltation was a kind of "begetting," of entering into the glorified rôle of the Son of God. Paul speaks of this same exaltation when he says that Christ was "designated Son of God in power . . . by his resurrection from the dead" (Rom. 1:4).

It is vigorously debated whether Jewish writers ever spoke of the expected Messiah as "Son of God." A few sayings can be found which suggest the possibility (Enoch 105:2, IV Ezra 7:28-29; 13:32; 14:9); but since we do not possess these writings in their original languages, it is uncertain what words were used.

This survey of the historical background of "Son of God" should suggest that the meaning of the term as used in the Gospels cannot be determined by theological presuppositions but only by careful inductive exegetical study. In such a study, theological presuppositions do not only seriously influence the conservative student but also the liberal critic. The former may, according to his presuppositions, insist that "Son of God" always means "God the Son"; but the latter may, according to his presuppositions insist that, since "history" can know nothing about incarnate deity, all alleged sayings of Jesus which seem to claim deity cannot be authentic but must have been placed in His mouth by later Christian faith. From such a humanistic understanding of history, the "historical Jesus" could never have made such claims as the Fourth Gospel records; it must be at this point quite unhistorical.

Both of these approaches are uncritical and unscientific. Scientific exegesis must deal inductively with the sources and not decide in advance what the results of the study will be. When such an inductive study of the term "Son of God" in the Gospels is made, the conclusion emerges that Jesus considered Himself to stand in a relationship to God which set Him apart from all other men. The language of the Synoptic Gospels confirms the implication of John 20:17: "I am ascending to my Father and your Father, to my God and your God." God is the Father of Jesus and Jesus is God's Son in a relationship which cannot be shared by other men. He is *uniquely* the Son of God, not in a creative, religious, or messianic sense, but in some profoundly personal sense which the Gospels do not expound. Matthew 11: 27 affirms that Jesus is related to the Father in the same way that the Father is related to Jesus: in a direct, unmediated, personal fellowship. In other words, Jesus used the term "Son of God" which was capable of various meanings and poured into it a new content to describe His own unique person and relationship to God. A contemporary critical scholar, recognizing this, has written that the historian as historian must recognize that Jesus claimed in some real sense to be divine.[1] The historian cannot decide whether this is a true claim; that is the task of theology.

The uncritical reader of the Gospels usually fails to understand that the messianic expression "Son of Man" viewed in its historical setting is even more important than "Son of God." To the uncritical reader, "Son of Man" designates the humanity of the God-man as "Son of God" means His deity. When interpreted historically, the question must be raised whether the background for the term is Ezekiel 2:1, where Ezekiel is addressed as a representative man (see Psalm 8:4), or Daniel 7:13, where "one like a son of man" is a heavenly figure representing the people of God who comes with the clouds to receive from God dominion over all the earth. We have some help in the second part of a Jewish writing called the "Similitudes of Enoch," which was approximately contemporary with Jesus. In this Jewish apocalypse, the Son of Man is a distinct individual of heaven-

---

[1] Vincent Taylor, *The Person of Christ in the New Testament Teaching* (New York: Macmillan [1958], p. 186).

ly, supernatural origin who pre-existed in heaven with God and is the agent of the establishment of God's Kingdom on earth.[2] Although we cannot establish the authorship or the exact date of this work, it is quite certain that we find here what the "Son of Man" meant to first-century Jews: not a humble man among men, but a heavenly, pre-existent, exalted being who would come to earth in glory to right all wrongs and establish the Kingdom of God.

This meaning of the Son of Man in Daniel 7 as a heavenly pre-existent being is the sense in which Jesus used the term. While there is no evidence that Jesus was acquainted with the Similitudes of Enoch, we must conclude that Jesus used the term in basically the same sense as Enoch, a sense which is derived from Daniel's use of the term. He Himself will be this heavenly Son of Man who is destined to decide the destiny of men (Mark 8:38; 14:62). However, before He comes in glory as the heavenly Son of Man, He has appeared on earth in humility among men to fulfill a mission of suffering and death. It is this heavenly Son of Man who is to be rejected by the leaders of the Jews (Mark 8:31), to be treated with contempt (Mark 9:12), to be delivered into the hands of men to be put to death (Mark 9:31), to be mocked, spit upon, scourged, and killed by Gentile hands (Mark 10:33, 34). However, this tragic death was no mere historical accident; it was the fulfillment of the mission of the Son of Man to give His life a ransom for many (Mark 10:45). Here, as the serving and suffering Son of Man, Jesus stands quite apart from Judaism. There is nothing like this in Enoch.

Thus in Jesus' use of the title "Son of Man," there is a veiled claim. By this title, Jesus claimed to be a supra-human heavenly being who will decide the destiny of men in the last judgment. But this claim was a veiled one, because the Jews had never heard of the Son of Man appearing on earth as a man among men to serve and minister, much less to suffer and die. How was it possible for a heavenly supernatural being, the final judge of

2 This apocalypse can be read in R. H. Charles, *The Apocrypha and Pseudepigrapha of the Old Testament in English* (Oxford: Clarendon, 1913).

all men, to be put to death at the hands of wicked men? This was quite confusing to first-century Jews. Thus when Jesus as the Son of Man claimed authority to forgive sins (Mark 2:10), to be lord of the Sabbath (Mark 2:27-28), yet to be homeless (Matthew 8:20; Luke 9:59), the title carried great significance. By its use Jesus designated His own heavenly, supernatural character, origin, and destiny, yet He was one destined to achieve His exalted role by humility, weakness, suffering, and death.

We have illustrated the important principle of historical criticism: that an interpreter cannot lift the concepts found in the New Testament out of context and impose any dogmatic interpretation on them that suits his interest. The New Testament must be interpreted in terms of its historical contexts. However, this fundamental principle itself must not be applied too rigidly. Room must be left for originality and creativity in the New Testament message. On a purely human level, a teacher can transcend his environment with original and novel insights; this is particularly important in the matter of the divine self-revelation.

The difficulty in deciding how far this principle of historical criticism should be applied can be illustrated by one of the best studies on the parables of Jesus that has been made.[3] Jeremias can be described as a "moderate" form critic, since he, in contrast to the Bultmannians, thinks that by the exercise of form criticism, he can recover the living voice of the historical Jesus.[4] As a form critic, he believes that the parables in their present form have their *Sitz im Leben* in the life of the Christian church, not the ministry of Jesus. He lists several literary principles that can be detected in the process of the transformation of the form of the parables from their original historical form as Jesus gave them to their present form in the life of the church. By applying these principles, he attempts to recover their original

[3] Joachim Jeremias, *The Parables of Jesus* (New York: Scribner's, revised ed. 1963).

[4] See his essay, "The Present Position in the Controversy Concerning the Problem of the Historical Jesus," *Expository Times*, 69 (1957-58), pp. 333-39.

literary form. In the application of the principles of form criticism, Jeremias again and again asks the question: "How would Jesus' Jewish audience have understood this parable?" He takes this as the controlling principle in recovering the original historical setting.

However, what Jesus' Jewish audience would have understood and what Jesus intended may not be the same. It is altogether too restrictive a critical principle to make first-century Jewish thought the norm for interpreting the parables. The *Sitz im Leben* of the parables is to be sought not in first-century Judaism but in the distinctive message and mission of Jesus.

We may illustrate this by the parable of the four soils (Matt. 13:3-9). Jeremias thinks that the parable in its present form is a Christian allegory describing the working of the gospel in the world.[5] The historical *Sitz im Leben* was the expectation of an imminent apocalyptic catastrophe. In this parable, Jesus gave the "great assurance" that in spite of every failure, the apocalyptic consummation of the Kingdom was certain.

However, Jeremias himself recognizes that Jesus taught not only a future apocalyptic coming of the Kingdom but also its presence in His own mission. This "mystery of the Kingdom," its presence in a historical event before its apocalyptic consummation, was something unheard of in Judaism; but it is the heart of Jesus' message and provides the *Sitz im Leben* for the parables of Matthew 13. The parable of the soils teaches that the Kingdom of God is present in Jesus' words, but like seed sown in the ground it requires a response by its recipients to be fruitful and effective.[6] This truth would not be readily understood by Jesus' Jewish audience, for the coming of the Kingdom of God was by definition an apocalyptic event which required no human response. It was the act of God alone, before which no

---

[5] An allegory is an artificial story whose details convey spiritual truth; a parable is a story drawn from life which teaches a single central truth, with details only providing "local color."

[6] See G. E. Ladd, "The *Sitz im Leben* of the Parables of Matthew 13: The Soils" in *Studia Evangelica*, ed. by F. L. Cross (Berlin: Akademie, 1964), II, 203-10.

man could stand. However, the mission of Jesus embodied a new redemptive event: The Kingdom *has come* (Matt. 12:28) into history in the person and mission of Jesus before its apocalyptic consummation.[7] This was not understood by most of the Jews, but only by Jesus' disciples, for its understanding required the response of personal faith (Matt. 13:11-17).

We have illustrated the necessity of historical criticism by a rather simple question in Paul's letters and by the very involved question of the meaning of the messianic terminology used by our Lord; and we have pointed out that this method cannot be applied too rigorously as Jeremias does in his interpretation of the parables. We must now turn to the most important question with which historical criticism has to deal: the problem of the so-called "historical Jesus." This has been the constantly recurring problem in historical criticism since the rise of rationalism and the emergence of the historical-critical method; in recent years it has assumed new proportions of significance.[8]

In introducing this question, we must recognize that the historical-critical method, as the discipline is employed by many critics, means far more than the method which we have thus far discussed: the interpretation of the Bible in its historical setting. "Historical criticism" often includes a distinct theology of the nature of history, including biblical history, which is alien to an evangelical understanding of redemptive history and revelation. This must be realized, even if it cannot be accepted.

The apparently elementary question must be raised: What is history? It requires only a bit of reflection to realize that history in any meaningful sense for the modern man cannot designate simply what happened in the past. We have no knowledge of what happened in the past apart from records, documents, and

---

[7] This thesis is worked out in detail in the author's book, *Jesus and the Kingdom* (New York: Harper and Row, 1964), chapter IX, "The Mystery of the Kingdom."

[8] Schweitzer's *The Quest of the Historical Jesus* (London: Black, 1911) traces this quest up to the twentieth century, and James M. Robinson's *A New Quest of the Historical Jesus* (Naperville: Allenson, 1959) outlines the recent developments.

other historical sources. If we had no New Testament, we would
know almost nothing about Jesus of Nazareth, for we have no
other historical records from the first century which say anything
substantial about Him. We could infer from the existence of
the Christian church that such a person once existed, but we
could say very little about him. Thus history is impossible
without written records about events in history.

When we read ancient historical records, we find them filled
with alleged events which contradict the nature of observable
human experience. For instance, the two books of the Maccabees describe the events of the second century B.C. in Palestine.
First Maccabees is rather sober, straightforward history; and most
scholars accept it as an essentially trustworthy record of what
happened. Second Maccabees covers some of the same ground,
but is replete with supernatural apparitions, visions, and alleged
events which are not consistent with observed human experience.
When, for instance, Heliodorus, the representative of the Greek
king, Seleucus, came to Jerusalem to confiscate the treasures
which the Jews had stored in the temple, he was prevented by a
divine intervention.

> For there appeared to them a magnificently caparisoned horse,
> with a rider of frightening mien, and it rushed furiously at
> Heliodorus and struck at him with its front hoofs. Its rider was
> seen to have armor and weapons of gold. Two young men also
> appeared to him, remarkably strong, gloriously beautiful and
> splendidly dressed, who stood on each side of him and scourged
> him continuously, inflicting many blows on him. When he
> suddenly fell to the ground and deep darkness came over him,
> his men took him up and put him on a stretcher and carried him
> away (II Macc. 3:25-28).

Second Maccabees records a number of such alleged events. Did
they happen? Are they history? Practically all Protestant scholars, liberal and conservative, exercise critical judgment on such
records and consider them the product of devout imagination,
not sober history.

Practically all ancient records contain such elements of imagination and legend, mythology and superstition. "History,"

therefore, must be defined as the *critical study of ancient records,* by which the modern scholar reconstructs what he thinks happened in the past.

This modern scientific study of history rests upon a certain presupposition about the nature of historical experience which excludes the reality of divine interventions. This is unambiguously expressed by one of the modern New Testament scholars, Rudolf Bultmann.

> The historical method includes the presupposition that history is a unity in the sense of a closed continuum of effects in which individual events are connected by the succession of cause and effect. This does not mean that the process of history is determined by the causal law and that there are no free decisions of men whose actions determine the course of historical happenings. But even a free decision does not happen without cause, without a motive; and the task of the historian is to come to know the motives of actions. All decisions and all deeds have their causes and consequences; and the historical method presupposes that it is possible in principle to exhibit these and their connection and thus to understand the whole historical process as a closed unity.
>
> This closedness means that the continuum of historical happenings cannot be rent by the interference of supernatural, transcendent powers and that therefore there is no "miracle" in this sense of the word. Such a miracle would be an event whose cause did not lie within history. . . . It is in accordance with such a method as this that the science of history goes to work on all historical documents. And there cannot be any exceptions in the case of biblical texts if the latter are at all to be understood historically.[9]

We must acknowledge that everyone uses this approach in his study of most of ancient history. But when this scientific approach is applied to the Bible, it results in serious problems. There is, for instance, according to the New Testament witness, no "historical" explanation for the resurrection of Jesus from the dead; it is a direct, unmediated act of God, without "historical," that is, human explanation, and without historical anal-

[9] *Existence and Faith,* ed. by Schubert M. Ogden (New York: Meridian Books, 1960) , pp. 291f.

ogy. The resurrection of Jesus is represented not as the return
of a dead body to physical, mortal, human life, but the emergence of eternal life within history (II Tim. 1:10). According
to Paul it is the first stage in the resurrection of the dead unto
eternal life which will occur at the end of human history (I Cor.
15:12-26). It is a miracle, not in the sense that it is a violation
of the laws of nature and human history, but in the sense that
it is the appearance within history of a higher order that transcends the world of nature and history — the realm of eternal
life which belongs to the world to come.

To this, Bultmann, speaking as a scientific historian, can only
answer, "An historical fact which involves a resurrection from
the dead is utterly inconceivable."[10] All such alleged events
are mythology, not history for a scientific historian like Bultmann. They are the expression of Christian faith in mythological terms, not a sober account of what happened. History at-
tests that death is the end of human existence on earth.

When this scientific approach is applied to the Gospels as
a whole, a similar problem arises, for the Jesus of the Gospels
is not a figure who can be explained in historical terms. He is
depicted as a sinless one; and sinlessness is not a human category. He is depicted as possessing a consciousness of deity; but
deity is not a historical category. He is depicted as one born
by a creative act of the Holy Spirit in the body of Mary; but
history cannot explain a virgin birth. He is depicted as one
possessing supernatural knowledge and supernatural power;
but such traits are not human, historical categories. He is depicted as one who willingly gave His life to redeem men from
sin; but history cannot explain how one man's death in Palestine
two thousand years ago can have saving efficacy for men of all
ages in all the world. He is depicted as God incarnate in the
flesh; but history can only relegate such ideas to ancient mythology which frequently conceived of the gods entering into
human affairs — events which the sober historian cannot ac-

10 *Kerygma and Myth*, ed. by H. W. Bartsch (New York: Harper and
Row, 1961), p. 39.

cept as factual. In other words, the essential portrait of Jesus found in our Gospels is "unhistorical" in this scientific sense, in that it completely transcends historical categories, cannot be explained in terms of historical causality, and is quite without historical analogy. Käsemann expresses this viewpoint clearly. In the Gospels, Jesus' words and deeds become "an unbroken series of divine revelations and mighty acts, which have no common basis of comparison with any other human life and thus can no longer be comprehended within the category of the historical."[11]

This is what is meant by the "historical Jesus" which is the center of much modern study and discussion. The "historical Jesus" is a technical term, designating not Jesus as He actually may have existed in history but a reconstruction of Jesus which is capable of being understood and explained in scientific, historical, purely human categories. Bultmann's entire theological effort can be described as an effort to find Christian meaning in a gospel which is expressed in unhistorical, mythological categories, which he, as a scientific historian, cannot possibly accept as real events.[12] The portrait of Jesus in the Gospels is shot through and through with mythological, that is, supernatural elements which defy history.

In the face of this conflict between the modern understanding of history and the portrait of Jesus in the Gospels, the critic is limited to several alternatives. We have already seen (above, pp. 142ff.) that the historical Jesus of old liberalism did not stand the test of subsequent criticism, and really existed neither in Mark nor Q, but only in the liberal critical reconstruction. Schweitzer's sketch of the historical Jesus in terms of first-century Jewish apocalyptic leaves Jesus with no relevance for modern faith; for it lets Jesus die on the cross in frustration, despair, and disillusionment. In response to the "unhistorical"

11 *Essays on New Testament Themes* (Naperville, Ill.: Allenson, 1964), p. 30.
12 See the present author's book, *Rudolf Bultmann* (Chicago: Inter-Varsity Press, 1964).

character of the Gospels, Bultmann ends in historical agnosticism. He believes that Jesus lived and died, and he knows a little about what Jesus did and said; but when asked to describe the person of Jesus, Bultmann can only answer, "I do indeed think that we can now know almost nothing concerning the life and personality of Jesus."[13]

This radical, consistent skepticism has disturbed Bultmann's followers, and they have launched a "new quest of the historical Jesus" in which they are trying to discover new categories of history by which they can remain scientific historians and yet reconstruct a "historical Jesus" who is a substantial figure.[14] These scholars can recognize, no more than Bultmann, the objective acts of God in history.

A different alternative is to recognize that the nature of the Christian faith and the witness of the Scriptures demands a different view of history. While the historical method possesses general validity, there is one stream of history which transcends the competence of this method. If there is a personal, living God who has acted in history, the nature of His acts might be expected to be beyond "historical," natural human explanation. In the study of redemptive history, the strict historical method has limitations imposed upon it by its own presuppositions about the nature of history which render it incompetent to make anything but negative conclusions about the great events recorded in the Bible.

Is there such a God who reveals Himself in history? The historian cannot say, for God is not a historical character, even though He acts in history. He inhabits eternity. Did God become incarnate in the man Jesus Christ? The historian as a historian has no way to answer this question, for such an incarnation is without true analogy. Did God raise Jesus from the dead? The historian can only say that if such an event occurred, it is without historical explanation or historical causality and

13 R. Bultmann, *Jesus and the Word* (New York: Scribner's, 1934), p. 8.
14 Günther Bornkamm's *Jesus of Nazareth* (New York: Harper and Row, 1963), is the outstanding modern illustration of this.

analogy, and therefore he, as a historian, cannot affirm it. But this is *precisely what Christian faith affirms*: that in the resurrection of Christ an event occurred in history, in time and in space, among men which is without historical explanation or causality, but is a direct unmediated act of God. Indeed, *when the historian can explain the resurrection of Jesus in purely human terms,* those who hold anything like an evangelical faith will be faced with a problem of shattering dimensions.

This theological view of redemptive history is convinced that a strictly "historical Jesus" never existed, and that the resurrection is a "supra-historical" event.[15] The successful establishment of this position is not an easy task, for it requires an interaction between historical science and Christian faith. Faith does not, however, mean a leap in the dark, an irrational credulity, a believing against evidences and against reason. It means believing in the light of historical facts, consistent with evidences, on the basis of witnesses. It would be impossible to believe in the resurrection of Jesus apart from the historical facts of His death, His burial, and the witness of the disciples that they had met Him alive. Nor could faith in His bodily resurrection survive if the corpse of Jesus had been produced to refute the witness of His disciples. Faith can never contradict established facts. But faith means accepting the witness of the biblical authors to events which transcend the strict historical method.

This interaction between historical criticism and faith may be best illustrated by the resurrection. The historian, *as a historian,* is limited to two alternatives in dealing with the resurrection. He may take a position of neutrality, asserting simply that he does not know what happened, that if a resurrection actually occurred, he has no historical tools by which to prove it. As a historian, he can establish certain facts: Jesus was really dead and buried; His followers were crushed in despair;

15 We should note that many contemporary critics share the position here set forth about the supra-historical nature of Jesus and the resurrection, but do not share the view of the Bible held by the present author.

suddenly and (for the historian) inexplicably, their despair was transformed into radiant confidence in Jesus' resurrection; they were certain they had met Jesus, alive from the dead; and the entombed body of Jesus disappeared. The historian must also admit that historical criticism has not yet found an adequate historical explanation for these facts; that for the historian, the transformation in the disciples is an unsolved problem.[16] He must also admit that the view that Jesus actually arose from the dead would explain all the facts.

On the other hand, the historian may go further than to admit ignorance; he may flatly affirm that the resurrection could not and did not happen. This Bultmann does. Again, however, the resurrection faith, the certainty of the disciples that Jesus was alive again from the dead, is a fact of history; and those who deny that Jesus rose from the dead feel the pressure of trying to explain historically what caused belief in the resurrection. In one place Bultmann makes the amazing statement that how this faith arose is not of basic importance.[17] How can a historian say that it is of no historical importance to explain the alleged event which gave rise to the single most significant movement in Western history? In another place Bultmann says that the historian can only account for the rise of the resurrection faith in terms of the impact Jesus had made on His disciples, which in turn led them to experience subjective visions which convinced them He was alive.[18] However, it is clear that Bultmann feels embarrassment as a historian with the inadequacy of this subjective hypothesis, for on another occasion, he has defended the view that visions are not merely subjective experiences but are in reality objective encounters.[19]

[16] Leonhard Goppelt in his history of the apostolic age points out that the conduct of the disciples after Jesus' death is in fact without historical analogy. See *Die apostolische und nachapostolische Zeit* (Göttingen: Vandenhoeck & Ruprecht, 1962), p. 5.

[17] Rudolf Bultmann, *Theology of the New Testament* (New York: Scribner's, 1951), I, 45.

I, 42.

[18] R. Bultmann, *Kerygma and Myth* (New York: Harper and Row, 1961),

[19] Quoted by Helmut Thielicke, *ibid.*, p. 152.

The historian is in a much more comfortable position if he admits that something happened which defies historical explanation, which is in fact without historical analogy. On the other hand, the believer in the resurrection is in a more comfortable position if he admits that the resurrection is an event which transcends ordinary historical explanation because it involves an unmediated act of God in history. Indeed, the Gospels do not say that anyone saw Jesus rise from the tomb, as does, for instance, the apocryphal Gospel of Peter. Nor, as we have already noted, does the New Testament explain the resurrection as the resuscitation of a dead corpse, but as the appearance of eternal life within history (II Tim. 1:10), as the first stage of the eschatological resurrection at the end of the world (I Cor. 15:23-26). Such realities transcend ordinary historical experience.

However, the resurrection is consistent with the known historical facts; it is indeed the one adequate explanation for these facts, and it is the uniform witness of the New Testament writers that God did in fact raise Jesus from the dead. Therefore faith is not a leap in the dark in defiance of facts and evidences, but is consistent with known facts and rests upon witnesses.

In this chapter, we have tried to illustrate the nature of historical criticism. We have argued that since revelation has occurred in historical events, the student of the Bible must employ historical criticism to understand these events in terms of their historical setting. But we have also argued that the historical method must not be allowed to determine the nature of revelation, but that the concept of revelation must be achieved inductively from the Bible itself. Bultmann's view of history is such that he cannot conceive of God acting objectively in history, but only in human existence.[20] This view substitutes an existential philosophy for the biblical view of redemptive

[20] See the present author's essay, "What Does Bultmann Mean by the Acts of God?" *Bulletin of the Evangelical Theological Society* (Spring, 1962), pp. 91-97.

history. If revelation has occurred in historical events, it is
not surprising that there is a dimension in these redemptive
events which transcends the historical method; but Christian
theology must not allow the modern historian to dictate to him
the limits of its discipline.[21] On the contrary, Christian theology must recognize that the critical-historical method is a child
of rationalism and as such is based on a naturalistic world view.
The Christian gospel unavoidably carries an offense to this
world view, for, as a recent scholar has written, "The story of
Jesus of Nazareth, according to all traditional Christian understanding of it, is the story of the intervention of God in history."[22] But modern critical historiography simply has no room
for such interventions. Our quotation from the critical historian
Rudolf Bultmann (p. 183) makes this clear. Therefore, the
Christian theologian must insist that there is a dimension of
the actual, past, objective events which occurred in history
which goes beyond the presuppositions of modern critical
historiography.

The author is well aware that the position he is taking is
capable of being misunderstood and misinterpreted. Evangelicals have not greatly concerned themselves about the nature of
"history" but have been deeply concerned to preserve the full
reality and objectivity of Jesus — a concern which the author
shares. Some readers may feel that such statements as those
made in this chapter, namely, that a "historical Jesus" never
existed, is a surrender of an evangelical faith and a denial of
the reality of Jesus in history.

The question at stake is how the modern Christian is to relate his theological formulation and communicate with those
who do not share his Christian convictions. Is the Christian
theologian to construct his own definition of history and ask

21 This is a central thesis in T. A. Roberts, *History and Christian Apologetic* (London: S.P.C.K., 1960) .
22 Stephen Neill, *The Interpretation of the New Testament 1861-1961*
(London: Oxford, 1964) , p. 221.

the secular world to accept it? Or is the theologian to accept the basic validity of the modern secular understanding of history, and attempt to interpret his faith in terms which will at least communicate with those who do not share his faith? If the theologian is to demand that the secular world accept his definition of history, he is faced with a forbidding task; for the Christian insists that in redemptive history, events occurred which are truly unique and without historical analogy. Furthermore, regularity, continuity, and causality in human history are facts universally recognized and assumed, even by theologians, in the study of world history. Indeed, without such regularity and continuity, there could be no history, and any elements of discontinuity could not be recognized. Therefore, it would appear to be a better methodology to admit the basic validity of the prevailing scientific historical method, but to insist on its limitations at the point of redemptive history where God has entered history in self-revelation and redemption.

This problem is brought into focus by two recent books dealing with the problem of contemporary biblical interpretation. Stephen Neill[23] says, "It seems to be the case that the faith of the church stands or falls with the general reliability of the historical evidence for the life and death of Jesus Christ." We agree heartily with the intent of this statement. If historical criticism could establish that the great events of redemptive history did not occur, any evangelical faith would be impossible. If the historical critic could prove that Jesus never rose from the tomb, Christian faith would be shattered. Scripture itself affirms as much (I Cor. 15:12-19). The question is, what is *historical* evidence? Can historical criticism prove that revelatory, redemptive events have happened? Neill says in another place, "It is essential to the ministry of Jesus that it takes place within the framework of Jewish history. That it is the continuation and culmination of all those mighty acts of God in the

23 *Op. cit.,* p. 221.

past. . . ."[24] The question here is, how can the *historian* talk
about the mighty acts of God? "No one has ever seen God"
(John 1:18). It is of course true that the same verse goes on to
say, "the only Son, who is in the bosom of the Father, he has
made him known." This is the point on which we must insist!
The supreme revelation of God has occurred *in history,* in
Jesus of Nazareth. The question is, What is the nature of this
revelation? And what is its relationship to the prevailing understanding of history?

The Gospels themselves indicate that the revelation of God
in Christ was not a self-evident event which forced itself upon
all observers, an event analogous to the presence of the hated
Roman legions in the fortress of Antonia. Everyone had to
admit, whether he liked it or not, that in the person of Pilate
the power of Rome was present. The meaning of the nails
driven through Jesus' hands was not debatable. But when Peter
confessed Jesus' Messiahship, Jesus said, "Flesh and blood has not
revealed this to you, but my Father who is in heaven" (Matt.
16:17). Again He said, "Father . . . thou hast hidden these things
from the wise and understanding and revealed them to babes"
(Matt. 11:25). It is the witness of Scripture that only faith can
understand what happened in history; and modern historiography does not rest on faith but on critical analysis of ancient
sources. Thus, when Neill writes, "The historian, if he is a true
historian, knows that there are no rules,"[25] the present author
is unable to follow him. Probably what this sweeping statement
is intended to mean is that the historian, like the scientist,
must be open to any conclusions to which the historical evidences
point. However, the prevailing historical method *does* have
rules, and it appears to be a better strategy to acknowledge
them rather than to ignore them. So, when Neill again writes
that "Christianity is a historical religion *in every sense* in which

24 *Ibid.,* p. 282.
25 *Ibid.,* p. 280.

this expression can be interpreted,"[26] he appears to be guilty of ambiguity of expression, even though the idea expressed is sound. We heartily agree that a Bultmannian denial of the pastness, the objectivity, and the reality of redemptive events in history destroys the heart of the Christian faith. This is apparently what Neill means. The Christian faith rests firmly upon the recognition and understanding of events in history. However, the prevailing interpretation of history is in terms of a closed continuum of unbroken causality, and it is our central contention that this interpretation of history cannot understand the Christian gospel.

Therefore, Hugh Anderson appears to have grasped these issues more clearly when he says that Jesus cannot be known through scientific, historical criticism but only "through our receiving and responding to the apostolic testimony within the context of the community's life and faith and worship."[27] Again, "the historian can neither prove the Incarnation . . . nor bring us to a risen Lord."[28] The historian can, however, preserve the truth that our faith is rooted and grounded in a particular history and person and life; and even beyond this, historical evidence can imply that God is present and acting in history; but it cannot prove it. Only faith can grasp this implication.[29]

The crucial issues here are those of the reality and objectivity of redemptive events in the past, and of the nature and function of faith. If faith has only to do with the human soul (or human existence, as Bultmann would say) and God, the entire present discussion is irrelevant. But if faith is concerned also

[26] *Ibid.*, p. 342; our italics.

[27] Hugh Anderson, *Jesus and Christian Origins* (London: Oxford, 1964), p. 316.

[28] *Loc. cit.* I have deliberately omitted a second element in Anderson's statement with which I cannot agree: "nor show us an empty tomb." I am convinced that the empty tomb, in spite of Anderson's learned discussion, is a sound historical fact and must be taken into consideration as one of the evidences pointing to the nature of the resurrection. See the author's essay on "The Resurrection of Jesus Christ" in *Christian Faith and Modern Theology*, C. F. H. Henry, ed. (New York: Channel Press, 1964).

[29] *Ibid.*, p. 315.

with the recognition of the reality and meaning of God's saving acts in redemptive history, then we must insist that only the *believing* historian can adequately understand what God has done in history. This agrees with the witness of Scripture itself: "if you believe in your heart that God raised him from the dead, you will be saved" (Rom. 10:9).

CHAPTER VIII

Comparative Religions Criticism

IN THE PRECEDING CHAPTER, WE HAVE DISCUSSED THE USE AND THE limitations of the historical method in studying the New Testament. We must now outline one particular aspect of the historical method which has had great influence, particularly in Germany. It is called the *religionsgeschichtliche Methode,* or the study of the Hebrew-Christian religion in terms of the history of religions in general.

We have argued that the historical study of the Bible requires us to interpret it in terms of its historical setting. However, our discussion has made room for the element of uniqueness, and even for the factor of divine intervention. We have argued that while biblical concepts cannot be understood unless they are interpreted in terms of their religious and historical environment, the possibility can always exist that new content is poured into a familiar concept. We have tried to show that the messianic terminology of the Gospels — Messiah, Son of Man, Son of God — must be interpreted historically and that the theological content can be understood only in terms of this historical setting; but we have also showed that Jesus poured new content into each of these terms.

We have also discussed at length-the nature of the historical method, and have defended the position that redemptive history involves divine acts in history and that a naturalistic historical criticism is incapable of understanding and correctly interpreting biblical history; a historical-theological approach is necessary.

Both of these positions would be utterly offensive to exponents of the *religionsgeschichtliche Methode*. This method represents the most thorough-going application of a naturalistic historicism to the study of the Bible. It assumes that biblical religion, in both the Old and New Testaments, passed through stages of growth and evolution like all ancient religions, and in this evolution was heavily influenced through interaction with its religious environment. This method involves the consistent application of the principle of analogy to biblical religion: the history and development of biblical religion must be analogous to the history and development of other ancient religions. This method is not at all interested in the truth of the Bible or in revelation. Hebrew religion is studied simply as one of many ancient Near Eastern religions, and the religion of the early church is seen as a syncretistic movement which had its ultimate origin with the teachings of Jesus of Nazareth and which borrowed and blended important elements from the first-century Jewish and Graeco-Roman religions.

This approach was popularized in nineteenth-century scholarship by Julius Wellhausen in his *Prolegomena to the History of Israel*. Wellhausen treated Israel's religion not as the vehicle of divine revelation but as a religious development resulting from the outworking of evolutionary principles manifesting themselves in religious history. This approach stifled the study of biblical theology for an entire generation and resulted in the production of a plethora of books tracing the evolution of biblical religion. One of the most popular was Harry Emerson Fosdick's *A Guide to the Understanding of the Bible* (1938).

The method of comparative religions was motivated by certain philosophical presuppositions about the nature of history and religion, particularly the presuppositions of evolution and natural historical development. In this sense, it was anti-revelatory and anti-theological. Revelation and theology belong to the realms of philosophy and dogma, not history. The history of the Hebrew-Christian religion cannot embody absolute truth, but must be a development resulting from the religious genius of the Hebrews in interaction with their religious environment.

Our present concern must be limited to the illustration of this method of study in the New Testament. It is universally admitted that the New Testament faith had its origin with Jesus of Nazareth who, humanly, was a Jew who lived in Palestine and taught His fellow Jews. The old liberal theology had reconstructed the picture of Jesus and set Him forth as a great religious genius and personality who was distinctive in that He had experienced God as no other man had done, and who taught men to love God and one another. This portrait, compatible with late nineteenth-century German philosophy, was shattered in part by the reconstruction of Albert Schweitzer, who applied the principle of *Religionsgeschichte* to Jesus.

We know from contemporary Jewish literature that many Jews lived with vivid apocalyptic expectations. "Apocalyptic" is a term used to designate a certain type of expectation about the end of the world. Apocalyptic viewed the world as evil, as subject to demonic powers, as the scene of suffering, pain, affliction and oppression for the righteous. These evils came upon God's people not merely because of the power of pagan nations, but because evil spirits, demons, had taken possession of this world while the God of Israel had become a sort of absentee deity, allowing the demons to have their way. "This Age" was therefore irredeemably evil.

God, however, had not abdicated. He would presently arise from His heavenly throne, break into history to destroy the supernatural powers of evil, purge the world of all corruption and oppression, and so bring the entire natural order under His catastrophic judgment. Out of the ruins of the present order under divine judgment would emerge a new order so different that it could only be designated by the term "the Age to Come."

The four important elements in this Jewish apocalyptic view are: (1) This Age, completely abandoned to evil and therefore beyond redemption; (2) the Age to Come, a new and different order of redeemed existence; (3) the apocalyptic visitation usually described as the coming of a heavenly Son of Man with clouds of glory to judge This Age and inaugurate the Age to Come; (4) the imminence of this catastrophic event.

Schweitzer interpreted Jesus exclusively in terms of this apocalyptic hope. Jesus was no ethical prophet, teaching men to love God and one another; He was an apocalyptic preacher who was convinced the world was immediately to come to a catastrophic end, whose one mission was to prepare Israel for imminent judgment. His ethics were not ideals for universal human conduct, nor the will of God for men in history. They were an emergency ethic completely conditioned by the shortness of the remaining time, an "interim ethic" to prepare men for the impending judgment. Because the end was at hand, the usual guidelines of wisdom and sobriety had no place. Jesus believed that when the end came crashing into history, He, Jesus, would be elevated to the clouds and become the heavenly Son of Man.

This was Schweitzer's "historical Jesus": a Jewish apocalyptist who proclaimed an event which did not happen — and can never happen. Such a deluded Jewish apocalyptist, for Schweitzer, cannot be the source or basis of Christian faith. Schweitzer clearly says that the historical Jesus is an offense to the modern man, not the founder of his faith.[1]

In this interpretation of Jesus we have a vivid illustration of the *religionsgeschichtliche* approach: the historical Jesus must be pictured in terms of His religious environment, which Schweitzer concluded was Jewish apocalyptic. This interpretation has had a permanent influence on subsequent criticism, especially in Germany. In fact, what little Bultmann knows about

---

[1] A. Schweitzer, *The Quest of the Historical Jesus* (London: Black, 1911), p. 339.

the historical Jesus is essentially in agreement with Schweitzer's picture. Bultmann does, indeed, stand apart from Schweitzer in finding a contemporary existential significance in this apocalyptic proclamation of Jesus, and he substitutes existential decision for Schweitzer's interim ethics. But Bultmann and the "post-Bultmannians" believe that the historical Jesus was essentially a Jewish apocalyptist proclaiming the imminent apocalyptic end of the world. In these circles, the problem created for the early church by the fact that this apocalyptic event did not occur (the delay of the parousia — the coming of the heavenly Son of Man) was one of the determining factors in the development of early Christian theology.

This *religionsgeschichtliche* method is applied not only to Jesus but to the entire history of New Testament theology, particularly its Christology. The clearest illustration of this is Rudolf Bultmann. Bultmann has the ability and the honesty to express many of his critical methods with vivid clarity. We have earlier analyzed the method of *Formgeschichte*, which studies the Gospel tradition in its oral form before it was written down in our Gospels or their sources. The form critics try to reconstruct the history of the oral tradition and to recover the various stages of theological development. Bultmann, who is one of the most notable form critics, has clearly stated that the practice of form criticism must be carried out in terms of the presuppositions of *Religionsgeschichte*.[2] This means that all ideas about Jesus appearing in the New Testament from Jesus Himself through the early Jewish church in Jerusalem and the Gentile church in Antioch (Acts 11:19ff.) to Paul and John must be interpreted "historically" in terms of changing religious environments, particularly the movement of the church from the Jewish to the Gentile world.

To understand what this means, we need to recall the main steps in New Testament history. The story begins with John the Baptist and with the short ministry of Jesus of Nazareth

---

[2] R. Bultmann, *Existence and Faith,* Schubert M. Ogden, ed. (New York: Meridian Books, 1960) , pp. 52ff.

to the Jews of Palestine. After Jesus' death, His disciples gathered together in Jerusalem as a new movement within Judaism. For a few years — we know not how long — this primitive church was a thoroughly Jewish movement, with the one distinctive: Jesus of Nazareth was indeed the Jewish Messiah, and as such had been raised from the dead, exalted to God's right hand, whence He would return in power and glory. After a few years, persecution struck this messianic fellowship and many were scattered throughout Palestine. Acts 10 and 11 record the conversion of the family of a Gentile centurion, Cornelius; and Acts 11:19ff. tells of the establishment of a church beyond the confines of Judaism among Gentiles in the Greek city of Antioch of Syria. Later came Paul, who, although he had a Jewish background, became the great apostle to the Gentile world.

Here, then, are the main steps in the history of the early church: Jesus, the Jewish church in Jerusalem, the Gentile church in Antioch, Paul the missionary and theologian of Gentile Christianity.

Bultmann maintains that the New Testament as we possess it, particularly the Gospels and Acts, are not historically accurate and do not correctly record the stages of theological[3] development from Jesus through the Jewish to the Gentile church. These books were written at a time so far removed from the history they record that they lost touch with the actual situation and obscured the stages of historical development. Therefore exegesis of the Gospels and Acts cannot engage in an inductive analysis of these records as they stand; it must attempt a historical reconstruction on the basis of the presuppositions of *Religionsgeschichte*. The Gospels and Acts reflect a later period, when Christian faith in Christ as the Son of God and divine redeemer had infused the true history. The critical historian is guided by critical principles that he is certain determined the historical development; and the New Testa-

---

[3] It would be more accurate to say "mythological" development for reasons which will shortly appear.

ment, especially the Gospels and Acts, must be critically analyzed in terms of these presuppositions.

This means, in brief, that the preaching of Jesus and the
faith of the Jewish church must conform to Jewish apocalyptic;
while the faith of the Gentile church must be understood in
terms of entirely different religious concepts which are derived
from the environment of pagan religions.

In applying this method, Bultmann agrees with Schweitzer
that Jesus was a Jewish apocalyptist preaching the imminent
end of the world. The primitive Jewish church in Jerusalem
had the same basic faith which centered in the expectation of
the imminent apocalyptic consummation. The chief difference
between Jesus' message and the faith of the early church is that
Jesus proclaimed the coming of some unknown heavenly figure
— the Son of Man — to bring to pass the end of This Age and
the inauguration of the Age to Come, while the early church
identified Jesus with this heavenly Son of Man. Both Jesus
and the primitive church are to be understood in terms of the
Jewish apocalyptic hope, which Bultmann calls a mythology,
for it does not consist of historical or objective events, but of
imagined heavenly events which the modern man knows are
fantasies. Jesus announced the coming of a heavenly being, to
bring the Kingdom of God, while the early church believed
that He had been exalted to heaven and would Himself come to
earth as Son of Man to bring to pass the apocalyptic consummation.

This reconstruction does not, of course, agree with the witness
of Acts. Luke records that the early church in Jerusalem believed that Jesus had been exalted to heaven and was therefore
worshipped as present *Lord and Messiah* (Acts 2:36). They did
indeed await His return (Acts 3:20), but the apocalyptic hope
was not the center of their proclamation. Rather, they preached
a Jesus who had been enthroned at the right hand of God, and
who therefore should be worshipped as the heavenly Lord. In
fact, in the early chapters of Acts, "Lord" is used interchange-
ably for God and for the exalted Christ.

Confronted with the witness of Acts, Bultmann believes that the reports preserved in Acts were so distorted by later Christian faith that they are historically untrustworthy. The modern critic using *Religionsgeschichte* can reconstruct what happened historically.

The book of Acts records that when Jewish believers who spoke Greek were scattered throughout Palestine and Syria, a church was established in Antioch consisting primarily of Gentiles (Acts 11:20) rather than Jews. The New Testament tells us almost nothing about this first Gentile church; but Bultmann is confident that here, on Gentile soil, the Christian faith assumed new form. The Jewish apocalyptic mythology about the end of the world, the coming of a heavenly Son of Man and the inauguration of the Age to Come would not be meaningful to Gentiles. We cannot think that they would have taken over the Jewish proclamation about the risen and exalted Jesus who would shortly come with glory as the Son of Man. However, the converted Gentiles had their own religious mythologies which they brought with them from their pagan worship. Gentile converts must have interpreted Jesus in terms of their own religious background.

Prominent in the Graeco-Roman world were the so-called mystery religions from which Bultmann thinks some of the Christians in Antioch had been converted. These mystery religions were oriental cults of personal salvation. They had arisen in the Near East, were brought into the West by slaves, merchants, and soldiers, and had taken deep root in the Graeco-Roman world. The cult of Attis and Cybele developed in Asia Minor, Isis and Osiris (Serapis) in Egypt, Adonis in Syria, and Mithraism later came from Persia. Originally these were national or tribal cults based on the yearly cycle of nature with its endless wheel of life and death.

In New Testament times, these cults had been divorced from their native soil and had become religions of personal redemption. Each of them was built around a myth of a god who died and rose again. In the ritual of these cults, the worshippers engaged in certain religious acts, by the performance of which they were mystically identified with the cult deity and made to share his life, thus obtaining immortality. These cult deities were looked upon as Lord by the initiates of the given cult and were addressed as *kyrios* (Lord).

Bultmann believes that when Gentiles in Antioch became Christians, they were able to understand the proclamation of the death, resurrection, and ascension of Jesus, for they were familiar with the idea of dying and rising gods in their pagan religious background. Therefore, they simply interpreted the death and resurrection of Jesus in terms of their former pagan beliefs, transforming Him in effect into a pagan cultic deity. The great difference, of course, was that it was an actual historical person, Jesus, who had been so exalted as Lord, not a shadowy figure of ancient nature myths. It was in this Gentile environment that Jesus became a heavenly cultic being. In Antioch for the first time Jesus was interpreted in terms of the oriental mystery cults and was believed to be not basically the apocalyptic Son of Man of the Jewish myth but a heavenly cultic deity of pagan mythology.

In this way Jesus came to be Lord. In the Jewish church, Jesus was not worshipped, nor was He thought of as Lord. He was believed to be the heavenly Son of Man whose coming was awaited. In the Greek (Hellenistic) church, Jesus came to have an entirely new significance. He was worshipped in the Christian cult as a present heavenly Lord to whom the worshippers looked for blessing and salvation, as they had formerly looked to their pagan cultic deities. Acts says that in Antioch the disciples were for the first time called Christians. Bultmann would add that in Antioch Jesus was for the first time called Lord.

There was a third mythology which Bultmann believes greatly influenced the history of New Testament thought as it developed in the Greek world — the mythology of Gnosticism. Gnosticism emerged in the second century A.D., especially in the Alexandrian church, as a heretical development with an elaborate

theology and an extensive literature. Gnosticism has been understood classically as an aberration of Christian theology resulting from the interpretation of the gospel in terms of Greek
dualism. This dualism differed from Jewish temporal dualism,
for it conceived not of two ages but of two worlds: the world
of matter and the world of spirit, below and above, darkness
and light. In this cosmological dualism, the world of the material is the realm of darkness, evil, sin. God stands over against
the world and must be thought of in complete contrast to fallen
matter. Man belongs to both worlds. He is both body and
spirit. As body, he is part of the fallen world of matter and
darkness; but in him is also the spiritual element, a spark of
light, the divine imprisoned in the body.

In second-century Gnosticism, Jesus was described as having
come from the realm of light to redeem man in order to enable
man to escape from the world of darkness and matter and to
return to the realm of light where He really belonged. This redemption Jesus accomplished not by death or suffering, but
through the impartation of knowledge (*gnosis*: whence "Gnosticism"). In Gnostic theology, Christ as a divine being neither
assumed a truly human body, nor did He die. He either tem-
porarily inhabited a human being, Jesus, or assumed only a
phantasmal human appearance. The influence of incipient
Gnostic ideas denying the reality of the incarnation is reflected
in John's insistence that Jesus has come in the flesh (I John 4:
1-3; cf. 1:1-2). The denial of a real fleshly incarnation is heretical.

Although Gnosticism is a historical phenomenon appearing
in the second century A.D., one school of German criticism, the
religionsgeschichtliche Schule, postulates a pre-Christian origin
for Gnostic ideas. These scholars believe that the appearance
of the Gnostic heresy in the second century was not simply the
result of the interpretation of Christ in terms of Greek dualistic
ideas. On the contrary, it was only a late development in a process which had been going on for several centuries in the Near
East. Before Jesus of Nazareth lived and died, there had al-

ready developed the mythology of a heavenly redeemer who comes from the realm of light to the fallen world to release sinful man and restore him to the realm of light whence he had fallen. This idea, according to Bultmann and the comparative religions school, does not reflect the facts of the Christian gospel, nor is it distinctively Christian, but belongs to pre-Christian oriental dualism. The New Testament's presentation of Jesus as a pre-existent divine being who becomes incarnate for man's redemption is not really Christian, but results from the interpretation of the historical Jesus in terms of the pagan dualistic Gnostic mythology.

At this point Bultmann makes his biggest leap. He postulates a conflation of the mystery redemption myth and the Gnostic myth as background for New Testament thought. The idea of a dying and rising cult deity (mystery religions) was conflated with the idea of a heavenly redeemer who comes to earth to save fallen man (Gnostic religion). These two were in turn added to the Jewish myth of a heavenly Son of Man. Out of this threefold conflation of Jewish apocalyptic, mystery, and Gnostic myths emerged the syncretistic figure of a heavenly being who comes from the realm of light to bring men the knowledge of God (Gnostic), who dies and rises again (mystery), who ascends to heaven and will come again as the Son of Man to break off history and inaugurate the Kingdom of God (Jewish apocalyptic). The fully developed Pauline Christology embodies all of these elements. Jesus of Nazareth, a Jewish apocalyptic prophet, has been transformed into a pre-existent divine being who becomes an incarnate revealer, a dying and rising Saviour, an enthroned heavenly Lord, and a coming Son of Man. The New Testament doctrine of Christ is thus the result of the transformation of a Jewish prophet into a syncretistic figure, the components of which are drawn partly from Jewish but mostly from pagan religious myths.

Bultmann's historical reconstruction of New Testament Christology, just outlined, is the most notable illustration from contemporary criticism of the thorough-going application of the *religionsgeschichtliche* method to the interpretation of the New Testament. It is obvious that in such an interpretation the traditional Christian doctrines of the pre-existence of Christ, the incarnation, His resurrection and ascension, His present lordship, and His coming in glory to establish the Kingdom of God are reduced to ancient mythologies or religious imagination which cannot be understood as realities or events in time and space. Bultmann does not, like the rationalists and liberals before him, simply discard these ancient mythologies and base his Christian confession on what is left of verifiable history; he "demythologizes" these ancient imaginary forms; i.e., he reinterprets them, trying to find a *meaning* which is not mythological but which can be understood in terms of a modern existential philosophy. He insists that it is not the imaginary form but the meaning in these mythologies which is important, and this meaning is concerned with personal existence, not with objective acts of God in history.[4]

The important thing which we must emphasize here is that this reconstruction is not only based on a philosophical presupposition about the nature of history and religious development rather than on inductive interpretation of our records; it is also contradicted by the New Testament itself. For this reason, this extreme form of criticism has not been popular in modern scholarship except in certain circles in Germany. In fact, the assumptions of this thorough-going *religionsgeschichtliche Methode* do not characterize the prevailing mood in biblical studies. In the last few decades, a more open-minded scholarship than that of Bultmann and his followers has recognized that neither the Old nor the New Testament can be adequately understood in terms of their religious environments but that both contain genuinely unique elements.[5] The central trend in New Testament studies, which is quite conservative in contrast to Bult-

---

4 See the author's book, *Rudolf Bultmann* (Chicago: Inter-Varsity, 1964).
5 See G. Ernest Wright, *The Old Testament Against Its Environment* (Naperville: Allenson, 1950) ; F. V. Filson, *The New Testament Against Its Environment* (Naperville: Allenson, 1952) .

mann, is reflected in two comprehensive recent studies, both by British theologians: Hugh Anderson's *Jesus and Christian Origins*[6] and Stephen Neill, *The Interpretation of the New Testament 1861-1961*.[7] Anderson's book is concerned with the critical problem of "the historical Jesus" in contemporary criticism, while Neill devotes more attention to the history of New Testament criticism, as his title suggests, primarily in Germany and Britain.

We can here indicate only a few exegetical facts which do not support Bultmann's *religionsgeschichtliche* reconstruction of New Testament history. In the first place, it is difficult to interpret Jesus simply in terms of first-century Jewish apocalyptic as Schweitzer and Bultmann have done. Increasingly, New Testament criticism is recognizing that while Jesus proclaimed a future apocalyptic event — the coming of the Kingdom of God, at the same time He proclaimed a divine event occurring within history in His own person and mission. "If it is by the Spirit of God that I cast out demons, then the kingdom of God *has come* upon you" (Matt. 12:28). The Kingdom of God is indeed a future apocalyptic, i.e., catastrophic event; but in some real sense, the Kingdom of God was present and active in history in Jesus' person, words, and deeds.

Secondly, the form in which the Gospels represent Jesus as having a consciousness of divine mission is such that it is difficult to see how a sober inductive exegesis can fail to recognize it. This is most evident in the use of the term "Son of Man." Bultmann believes that Jesus did not apply this term to Himself in any form but used it to designate the coming of a future apocalyptic heavenly personage. In the early Jewish church, the exalted Jesus was identified with this heavenly Son of Man; and in the Gospel tradition which was then preserved in oral form by the church, the term was put into the mouth of Jesus to designate Himself both in His future glory and in His

6 New York: Oxford, 1964.
7 New York: Oxford, 1964.

present humiliation and suffering. "Son of Man" in the Gospels represents Christian faith about Jesus, not the historical form of His teaching.

This critical conclusion, however, simply does not agree with the data of the New Testament. We have no evidence that the early church used the title "Son of Man." Outside of the Gospels many other titles are applied to Jesus. He is above all the Messiah or Christ (Acts 2:36; Rom. 9:5; Rev. 11:15), the Lord (Acts 2:36; Rom. 10:9; II Cor. 4:5; I Pet. 3:15), and the Son of God (Acts 9:20; Rom. 1:3; Heb. 4:14; I John 1:3); but He is also the Prophet (Acts 3:23; 7:37), the Servant (Acts 3:13, 26; 4:27, 30), the Saviour (Acts 5:31; Phil. 3:20; II Pet. 1:11), the High Priest (Heb. 2:17; 4:15), the Word (John 1:1-12), and on a few occasions at least He is even called God (Rom. 9:5; Tit. 2:13).[8] There is only one isolated place in the entire New Testament, outside of the Gospels, where the title "Son of Man" is applied to Jesus. When Stephen was dying he said, "Behold, I see the heavens opened, and the Son of Man standing at the right hand of God" (Acts 7:56). However, this is an isolated instance; and it refers neither to Jesus in the glory of His parousia, nor in His earthly humility and sufferings, but in His present exaltation at the right hand of God.[9]

Furthermore, the Evangelists do not apply "Son of Man" to Jesus; the title occurs only when Jesus is speaking. Although "Son of Man" occurs sixty-nine times in the first three Gospels, it is never the Evangelists' designation for Jesus, but only His self-designation.[10]

The significance of this fact can be appreciated when we note that the Evangelists use other titles. Mark introduces his Gos-

[8] See the excellent study by Vincent Taylor, *The Names of Jesus* (New York: St. Martin's, 1953).

[9] In Revelation 1:13, the exalted Jesus is described as "one like a son of man"; and in 14:14 "one like a son of man" is seen seated on a cloud. These are both obviously direct allusions to Daniel 7:13; "Son of Man" is not used as a title.

[10] This point is strongly made by Oscar Cullmann, *Christology of the New Testament* (Philadelphia: Westminister, 1959), pp. 155, 164.

pel by calling Jesus the Son of God (Mark 1:1); Matthew calls
Jesus the son of David, the Christ (Matthew 1:1, 17); and
Luke alone among the Evangelists, often refers to Jesus as the
Lord (Luke 7:13; 11:39; 13:15; 17:5), meaning, "Jesus, whom
we now know to be the Lord." Nowhere do the Evangelists in
their narrative material refer to Jesus as the "Son of Man."

The force of this fact is in no way weakened when one Evangelist attributes the title to Jesus when another does not.
Matthew 16:13 reads, "Who do men say that the Son of man
is?" while Mark 8:26 has, "Who do men say that I am?" Such
substitutions only reinforce the conclusion that the Evangelists
were conscious of preserving a true tradition, namely, that Jesus
alone used the title of Himself.

Finally, in the Gospels, Jesus' hearers never address Him as
the "Son of Man," unless in response to Jesus' own usage, as in
John 12:34.

It is therefore the consistent witness of the New Testament
records that "Son of Man" was a term used only by Jesus to
designate Himself; it was not a title used either by the early
church, nor by the Evangelists, nor by Jesus' disciples, nor
by the Jews. When historical presuppositions can lead the
scholar to ignore such clear and strong exegetical facts, it is
difficult to see how one can have any confidence either
in the integrity of the sources or in the validity of his
critical findings. If a sober, inductive criticism can establish
anything, it is that Jesus alone spoke of the suffering and the
glory of the Son of Man; and the idea of a heavenly Son of
Man who appears on earth in humility and weakness to suffer
and die was a novel idea which cannot be explained in terms
of the Jewish religious environment but only from Jesus' own
redemptive mission.

A third exegetical fact which contradicts Bultmann has been
called the "Achilles heel" of the *religionsgeschichtliche* reconstruction.[11] Bultmann, following Wilhelm Bousset, argues that

---

11 See A. E. J. Rawlinson, *The New Testament Doctrine of Christ* (London: Longmans, 1926), pp. 231-37.

Jesus could only be addressed and worshipped as heavenly Lord when He was interpreted by pagan converts in terms of the mystery religions' dying and rising cultic deities. In spite of Acts 2:36, in Jerusalem Jesus was known as the apocalyptic Son of Man, not as exalted heavenly Lord.

This theory is shattered by a single word in I Corinthians 16:22, "If any one has no love for the Lord, let him be accursed. Our Lord, come!"[12] Here is a prayer addressed to a Gentile Greek-speaking church which did not know the Aramaic language of Palestine, and it invokes the coming of the Lord Jesus. The fact that Jesus is called *Mar* (Lord) proves that this designation goes back to the earliest Aramaic tradition about Jesus. An idiom arising in the Greek churches would not make use of a meaningless Aramaic word. Thus the view that Jesus was not known as Lord by the Jewish church but only by the Greek church is contradicted by the exegetical facts of the New Testament. The designation by Jewish Christians of Jesus as Lord (*Mar*) became so deeply imbedded in their liturgical idiom that it could be carried over into Greek-speaking congregations with full religious meaning.

A fourth problem for the *religionsgeschichtliche* reconstruction will show the need of thorough historical scholarship. Bultmann holds that Jesus was finally interpreted in the Gentile world in terms of the Gnostic mythology of a pre-existent heavenly redeemer who descends to earth to deliver men imprisoned in the realm of fallen matter and to lead them back to the realm of light where they belong. It is, however, a fact that none of the ancient sources knows of such a heavenly redeemer in pre-Christian times.[13] Such an alleged figure is a critical hypothesis derived from post-Christian sources which

12 RSV. The Authorized Version has: ". . . let him be Anathema Maranatha." The RSV correctly puts a period between the last two words. The two Aramaic words *Marana tha* mean "Our Lord, come!"

13 See the authoritative study by R. McL. Wilson, *The Gnostic Problem* (London: Mowbray, 1958), p. 217.

were influenced by Christian faith. The historical fact is that "there is no hint of the figure of the redeemer in any non-Christian Gnostic source."[14] One of the main foundations of Bultmann's historical reconstruction is without firm historical support.

These serious weaknesses in the *religionsgeschichtliche* interpretation of the New Testament explain why this approach has not gained much favor outside the circles of "advanced" German criticism. Indeed, a recent British critic has expressed amazement that this school of criticism should ever have any serious influence outside its own circles.[15]

A different question is raised for the evangelical view of the Bible as the Word of God: Is not this entire approach to biblical criticism wrong-headed? If the Bible is the record of God's revelatory, redeeming acts in history, must we not conclude that revelatory history will be distinctive and unique at every point, and that we must always find differences, not similarities in comparison with the Semitic, Jewish and Hellenistic environments? But why should we expect everything to be distinctive and unique? Why could not God make use of rites, practices, even ideas from the ancient religious milieu as the vehicle for revelation?

As a matter of simple fact, this is what appears to have happened at numerous points. We may illustrate this by two basic cultic acts in Israel's religion: sacrifice and circumcision. Neither of these religious practices was unique to Israel. Practically all ancient religions engaged in animal sacrifice, and circumcision was a rite practiced by most all ancient Semitic peoples, the Egyptians being a notable exception. These two common cultic acts have been caught up in revelatory history and *infused with new content* so that their particular

[14] Hugh Anderson, *Jesus and Christian Origins* (New York: Oxford, 1964), p. 52.

[15] A. M. Hunter, *Interpreting the New Testament 1900-1950* (London: SCM, 1951), p. 218.

significance in the history of God's covenant with Israel becomes distinctive.

The extent of this kind of "borrowing" or adaptation of cultic acts and religious ideas demands careful attention by evangelical scholars. One point where this problem comes to sharpest focus is the relationship of New Testament thought to contemporary Judaism, on the one hand, and to the Old Testament Scriptures on the other. We have seen that Schweitzer interpreted Jesus not as an ethical prophet of God's love but as a first-century Jewish apocalyptist who proclaimed the end of the world, the coming of the heavenly Son of Man, and the inbreaking of the Age to Come. Was Schweitzer *altogether* wrong in this reconstruction?

The fact of the matter is that the idiom of our Gospels about this apocalyptic event is closer to contemporary Jewish apocalyptic at certain distinctive points than it is to the Old Testament. Jesus spoke about This Age and the Age to Come — a fact which is quite obscured in the Authorized Version. The Age to Come is the age of eternal life in the Kingdom of God (Mark 10: 29-30). The cares of This Age are hostile to the Kingdom of God and can choke its life (Mark 4:19). This Age will be brought to its end by the parousia of the Son of Man (Matt. 24:3), who will accomplish the judgment of men (Matt. 13: 39f.), separating the righteous from the wicked (Matt. 13: 49), and causing the righteous to inherit the Kingdom of God (Matt. 25:34). This antithetical structure of the two ages, divided by the coming of the Son of Man, provides the basic structure of New Testament redemptive history and theology.

The Old Testament does not use the language of This Age and the Age to Come, but contemporary Jewish apocalyptic literature does.[16] This fact has led one of the staunchest defenders of the evangelical faith in the last generation to the conclusion that both Jesus and Paul were led by the inspiring Holy Spirit to take over a piece of contemporary Jewish thought

[16] See Enoch 16:1; 48:7; 71:15; IV Ezra 7:50, 113; 8:1; Apoc. Baruch 14:13; 15:7; Pirke Aboth 4:1, 21; 6:4, 7.

and to imbed it in their revelatory teachings.[17] While this is true, the factors involved are far more complicated than this simple statement of the fact would suggest. The Jewish view of two ages, shared by the New Testament, appears to be a natural development of the Old Testament idea of the new order to be introduced by the eschatological visitation of God to establish His rule in the world. As Eichrodt has said, "The expected world-order is different in kind from the present one, and this long before the expressions 'the present age' and 'the age to come' had been invented."[18]

There are other rather obvious points where redemptive history in the New Testament has adopted contemporary historical phenomena. This appears to be true of Christian baptism. There is no adequate reason to doubt that Christian baptism in the early church was adapted historically from John the Baptist; and that he in turn had modeled his baptism after Jewish washings and ablutions. This is also true of the form of Christian worship. The early fellowship of Jewish believers was undoubtedly looked upon as a sort of Jewish synagogue, of which there were many in Jerusalem;[19] and the sudden unexplained appearance of elders in the Christian congregation (Acts 11:30) can easily be understood if the Jewish Christian fellowship imitated the example of the Jewish synagogue, with which it was familiar, of selecting a group of the oldest and most mature members of the congregation to provide leadership and order.

Such illustrations are not meant to defend the validity of the *religionsgeschichtliche Methode,* for this method of criticism rests upon a philosophy of the evolution of religion which has no room for the acts of God in revelation. We have only tried

[17] Geerhardus Vos, *The Pauline Eschatology* (Grand Rapids: Eerdmans, 1952), chaps. 1 and 2. The present author has discussed this problem in detail in his book, *Jesus and the Kingdom* (New York: Harper & Row, 1964).

[18] W. Eichrodt, *Theology of the Old Testament* (Philadelphia: Westminster, 1961), p. 491.

[19] Acts 6:9 may designate four different synagogues.

to indicate that reaction against this method ought not to lead one to the opposite extreme of denying any historical interaction or borrowing in redemptive history from the religious milieu. Good evangelical historical scholarship must endeavor by inductive historical criticism to discover both the points of similarity as well as dissimilarity between the Bible and the ancient world. If revelation has occurred in history, a sober scholarship should not make up its mind in advance what the facts are but should try to discover by careful examination where God has been pleased to make use of existing historical and religious phenomena, and where the Holy Spirit has impelled men to act and think creatively so that unique, distinctive factors emerge.

[20] An outstanding recent book by a thoroughly evangelical scholar seeks to determine how much of Paul's thinking about the law was carried over from his Jewish background and how much is due to his distinctive Christion experience. See R. N. Longenecker, *Paul Apostle of Liberty* (New York: Harper and Row, 1964).

Conclusion

THE PURPOSE OF THIS BOOK HAS NOT BEEN TO SOLVE ALL CRITICAL problems nor to give answers to numerous questions criticism must raise. Its purpose has been to show that an evangelical understanding of the Bible as the Word of God written is not *per se* hostile to a sober criticism; rather, an evangelical faith demands a critical methodology in the reconstruction of the historical side of the process of revelation.

Perhaps the book has raised more questions than it has solved. One may wonder how the critical method applies to a thousand other problems not discussed in this book. If so, then evangelical scholars must specialize in various areas of biblical criticism and creatively work through the historical questions. Evangelicals cannot be satisfied simply to recognize and defend the Bible as the Word of God; they must examine thoroughly the dimensions of the Bible as the words of men.

In such a study, we must constantly be reminded that the authority of the Bible which results from its recording and interpretative role in revelatory and redemptive history does not extend to these critical questions involved in the historical dimension of the Bible, unless this dimension is itself made the content of revelation. An evangelical criticism as well as a rationalistic criticism must often be satisfied with hypotheses, probabilities, possibilities, rather than in dogmatic certainties, as distasteful as this may be to the uncritical mind which insists on "thus saith the Lord" in every detail of Bible study. Such questions as the original ending of Mark, the precise meaning of δοκίμιον (see p. 89), the authorship of the first Gospel, the *Sitz im Leben* of the Gospel of John, the nature of the problem Paul faced in the church in Corinth (whether Jewish or Gnostic), the degree to which God in redemptive history has made use of elements from the Jewish and Hellenistic environments — all these do not constitute the content of revealed truth but are aspects of the historical media through which revelation has been given. Even when such questions cannot be satisfactorily answered, we possess God's revelatory Word which is an adequate and authoritative norm for Christian faith and practice.

This dual nature of the Bible is its most important characteristic: it is at the same time the Word of God and the words of men. Many theologians recognize that the Bible in some sense contains the Word of God, or is the vehicle of the Word of God, or witnesses to the Word of God; but it remains itself only the words of men. As a human book the truth taught in the Bible is not revealed truth but must be itself criticized by the Word of God which somehow comes through the Bible. The first chapter of this book gives reason for the conviction that the Bible is itself the Word of God, though expressed in the words of men, and that the truth taught in the Bible is one aspect of the normative and authoritative record and interpretation of revelatory, redeeming history. God acted in redeeming history, and God spoke through the prophets as they spoke and as they wrote. The result is not a mere product of history or religious insight; it is a normative, authoritative, divinely initiated and superintended account of who God has revealed Himself to be and what He has done for man's salvation.

Thus the Bible is indeed the inspired Word of God, the

Christian's only infallible rule for faith and practice. But the present study has attempted to demonstrate that the truth of infallibility does not extend to the preservation of an infallible text, nor to an infallible lexicography, nor to infallible answers to all questions about authorship, date, sources, etc., nor to an infallible reconstruction of the historical situation in which revelatory events occurred and the books of the Bible were written. Such questions God in His providence has committed to human scholarship to answer; and often the answers must be imperfect and tentative. A proper evangelical, biblical faith suffers a serious disservice when the spheres of biblical authority and critical judgment are confused.

Although the truth of the Bible is not dependent upon our ability to answer critical questions, it is quite clear that our understanding of the truth of the Bible is enlarged and rendered more precise by such study. A proper biblical criticism therefore does not mean criticizing the Word of God but trying to understand the Word of God and how it has been given to man. Some of the illustrations cited, particularly in the chapter on literary criticism, have indeed often been treated differently by evangelicals whose view of what infallibility ought to mean does not allow them to adopt conclusions such as those suggested in this book. However, as E. F. Harrison has pointed out, we must take into account all the facts of Scripture, both theological and phenomenological, in the formation of our doctrine of inspiration: "We may have our own ideas as to how God should have inspired the Word, but it is more profitable to learn, if we can, how he has actually inspired it."[1]

When all this has been said, one final point must not be lost sight of. The fact that the Bible is the living Word of God means that the layman need not wait for the scholar's interpretation before he can hear the saving message of the Scripture. It is to be hoped that the present study has not given the impression that the Bible must be a closed book to all but the scholar.

[1] See E. F. Harrison, "The Phenomena of Scripture," in *Revelation and Reason*, C. F. H. Henry, ed. (Grand Rapids: Baker, 1958), p. 249.

Although the Bible's message is conditioned by its historical setting, its character as the Word of God is manifested in the fact that it can be read by men of all times, of all races, of all cultural and educational levels and its redeeming message understood and believed.

The critical study of the Bible is necessary, not to grasp its saving power to speak to men of the redemption that is in Jesus Christ, or to bring them through Christ to God, but to answer questions about the historical process by which God has given us His Word. To be sure, there are innumerable places where the spiritual message of the Bible will be far better understood when its historical setting is disclosed, and for this reason the layman should constantly seek the aid of helps in biblical study prepared by good scholars; and scholars should not neglect the preparing of such scholarly but non-technical tools for laymen. However, it must not be forgotten that such critical study involves the effort to recover a complex historical process now often lost to us. Therefore the conclusions of scholars will often differ from each other; certainty often cannot be obtained. Nevertheless, critical study has shed a flood of light upon our understanding of the New Testament.

Here is perhaps the greatest miracle of the Bible: that in the contingencies and relativities of history God has given to men His saving self-revelation in Jesus of Nazareth, recorded and interpreted in the New Testament; and that in the New Testament itself, which is the words of men written within specific historical situations, and therefore subject to the theories and hypotheses of historical and critical investigation, we have the saving, edifying, sure Word of God. In hearing and obeying the Word of God, the scholar must take the same stance as the layman: a humble response which falls to its knees with the prayer, Speak, Lord, for thy servant heareth.

Index

219